Philosophy Updated

FOLLOW Hobbes Laws!

L. E. A.

1ST EDITION

NAPLES 2003

Philosophy Updated

✦

British Empiricism
Thomas Hobbes: The Laws of a Social Contract
John Locke: The Blank Slate of Our Minds
David Hume: Natural Religion and Human Nature

Selections and Commentary on Great Philosophers updated into modern, readable language for students of all ages.

Prof. Dr. Les Sutter

iUniverse, Inc.
New York Lincoln Shanghai

Philosophy Updated
British Empiricism Thomas Hobbes: The Laws of a Social Contract John Locke: The Blank Slate of Our Minds David Hume: Natural Religion and Human Nature

iUniverse, Inc.

For information address:
iUniverse, Inc.
2021 Pine Lake Road, Suite 100
Lincoln, NE 68512
www.iuniverse.com

ISBN: 0-595-28191-5

Printed in the United States of America

Contents

Introduction

As a Professor of Liberal Arts who primarily teaches Philosophy, Ethics, Logic, and Professional Ethics and Social Responsibility I am confronted by a common problem: how can I get my students to read the classic texts in Philosophy when they are so unreadable? In the textbooks I use in my classes, the authors try to be merciful and select fairly short, readable, edited versions of the originals. The best translations are chosen. Good introductions precede these readings, but all is somehow lost. The following week I am greeted by blank looks. They didn't read the selection at all, glanced through it, or suffered a severe headache and a crying spell trying to make sense of it all. The result is that some dislike Philosophy intensely, a subject they should love like wisdom itself.

Other professors will testify that too much time is spent in class explaining (some say spoon-feeding) students the texts they should have read and digested before arriving. I would take a more charitable view, because I don't have half the problem with selections on Existentialism because someone like Jean-Paul Sartre or Albert Camus speak to today's student very directly. Most students read the selections easily and arrive ready to discuss and argue the ideas and values imbedded. If this is the state of affairs, what can be done to make the "old" unreadable texts more approachable? What would facilitate a greater understanding of the core ideas without sacrificing a reading of the original?

I believe the answer lies in modernizing the dated texts with updated language along the same lines as "Good News for Modern Man" did for the Bible. Yes, it was controversial. Yes, it was imperfect. And yes, it was a major success because it reached its target audience. I plan to do the same. I expect a great deal of criticism. So be it. This updating is urgently needed and long overdue.

My method is straightforward: I have updated public domain translations or originals to modern, readable language for anyone interested in these Philosophers. I have taken extensive liberties in paraphrasing, abridging and editing selections of my choosing. Every chapter has a standard disclaimer: this is not the original—but the original is available—and good luck reading it!

A final comment: I spent some time as a German to English financial translator at a big Swiss bank, and can testify that no translation or editing job is ever perfect. In fact, a "perfect" literal translation can be a disaster; yet another flawless translation of Descartes or Hegel or Kant will not make them any easier to read. What is needed is a modern interpretation/paraphrasing/updating of these writings so they don't scare off the reader.

The task becomes improving communication and the free flow of ideas. I hope you find my updating useful.

Dr. Les Sutter

PART I
HOBBES

A Short Biography Thomas Hobbes (Born: April 5, 1588. Died December 4, 1679)

Thomas Hobbes was born prematurely in Westport, a village near Maimesbury as the Spanish Armada approached the English coast. He later claimed his metaphysical twin was 'fear' which caused him to 'seek peace' the first of his famous laws. His father permanently left Westport for London after an altercation with another minister on the church portal: Hobbes never saw him again. Raised with the aid of family members, especially a wealthy uncle, Hobbes entered Oxford at age 14.

As you will read, Hobbes wasn't impressed with the curriculum at English Universities and their reliance on the doctrines of Aristotle. This attitude, which he shares with Locke and Hume, led to rebellion and he spent most of his free time studying maps, developing an interest in science and trapping birds. In fact his boyhood friends dubbed him 'Crow' due to his raven black hair and love of birds.

Upon graduation Hobbes secured tutoring positions and traveled widely. Paris became his second home, but he loved England above all other nations. He was a secretary of sorts to Sir Francis Bacon, tutored the Prince of Wales (later King Charles II) and visited Galileo while under house arrest. His closest friend was said to be Pierre Gassendi, and Rene Descartes his worst enemy. Hobbes was on friendly terms with the top scientists of his day: Harvey, Boyle and other esteemed members of the Royal Society. Due to trumped up charges of Atheism against him, the Society never admitted Hobbes as a member, not so much out of fear, but simply from a dislike of political and theological intrigues brewing at the time. For political reasons, Hobbes returned to Paris in self-imposed exile for over a decade, only to flee back to England in 1651 on the heels of storm created by the publication of *Leviathan.*

His book inflamed both French Catholics and the English ex-patriot community, but luckily his former pupil, now King, welcomed 'The Bear' back to England. Charles loved to 'bait' Hobbes and relished his witty comebacks.

After a bout of plague, followed by the Great Fire of London in 1666, superstitious elements in Parliament proposed laws against religious and intellectual freedom, and for a time Hobbes' works were under fire, and had to published in tolerant Holland. In 1667, other restrictive laws were proposed, and if passed would have put Hobbes in prison; luckily they failed or were tabled.

Controversy hounded Hobbes until his death but he remained very end, but he remained active, arguing, disputing scientific and mathematical theories and publishing translations of the Iliad and the Odyssey at age 85. He died aged 91 in 1679; four years later *Leviathan* and *De Civi*, his principle works, were banned by Oxford University. He was buried in Ault Hucknall Church, Wardwick, England.

Selections from "Leviathan" by Thomas Hobbes, Updated, Edited and Modernized by Prof. Les Sutter (copyright of paraphrase, 2003)

LEVIATHAN

Introduction

Nature, the way God made and governs the world, is the way man imitates many other things, and is the way to make an artificial creature. Seeing life as nothing but a motion of limbs, the beginning is in some principal part. Couldn't we say that all automata (engines that move themselves by springs and wheels like a watch) have an artificial life? What is the heart but a spring? And the nerves, but so many strings? And the joints, but so many wheels, all giving motion to the whole body, such as was intended by the designer? This goes on even further, imitating that rational and most excellent work of nature, man. So, too, was the great Leviathan (the Biblical sea monster) we call a Commonwealth, or State created, which is nothing but a larger and stronger artificial man, created with the intention to protect and defend humanity. 'Sovereignty' is its artificial soul, giving life and motion to the whole political body. The magistrates, and other officers of judiciary are its artificial joints. Rewards and punishments are the nerves, that operate just as they do in a body natural; the wealth and riches of all various citizens are the strength. The people's safety, its business; counselors are the memory; equity, and laws, are an artificial reason and will; concord, health, sedition, sickness. And civil war is its death. Finally, the treaties and contracts, by which the parts of this political body were at first made and united, resemble that fiat, or man, pronounced by God in creation. To describe the nature of this artificial man, I will consider the following:

First: The substance and creator of the State, which is humanity.

Second: How, and by which laws, it is created. What are the rights and just power or authority of a sovereign? What it is that preserves or dissolves it?

Third: What is a Commonwealth?

Finally: What is a Kingdom of Darkness?

Concerning the first, there is a saying often used lately, that wisdom is acquired, not by reading of books, but of men. Consequently persons that offer no proof of being wise take great delight in showing what they think they know about men by backstabbing them. But there's another saying, currently misunderstood, by which they should learn to truly understand one another, if they would take trouble. It is *know thyself*. This was meant to teach the similarity of the thoughts and passions of men. When one looks inward and considers what he does when he thinks, forms opinions, reasons, hopes and fears, and why he does so, should thus know the thoughts and passions of all other men are on similar occasions.

I say similar *passions,* which are the same in all men (desire, fear, hope, etc.) not the similar *objects* of the passions, which are the things desired, feared, hoped, etc. These things vary, and they are so easily hidden that the character of man's heart, blotted by lying, counterfeiting, and erroneous doctrines, are legible only to those that question the human heart. And even though men's actions sometimes betray their plans; yet without comparing them with our own and examining all the circumstances, is to decipher without a code. One can be deceived by too much trust, or by too much diffidence because he reads others as he reads himself—a good or evil man.

But if one man reads another by his actions perfectly, it serves him only with his friends, which are few. He that governs a whole nation must read in himself, not this or that particular man, but mankind. This is hard to do, harder than to learn any language or science. For this kind of doctrine allows no other demonstration.

Part One: Of Man

CHAPTER I

Of Sense

I will first consider the thoughts of man singly, and then in a train of thought, or in their dependence upon one another. Singly, each one is a *representation* or *appearance,* of some quality, or other accident of a body external to us, which is commonly called an *object.* These objects work on the eyes, ears, and other parts of a man's body; and by a diversity of operations, produce diversity of appearances.

The first of these we call a 'sense', for no conception enters a man's mind, which isn't first either totally, or in part, grasp by our sensory organs. The rest are derived from the senses. To know the natural cause of sensation is not necessary for the question at hand; and I have written elsewhere about this at length. Nevertheless, to complete each part of my method, I'll briefly cover the subject below.

The cause of 'sense' is the external object that impresses the sensory organ, either immediately, as in taste and touch; or indirectly, as in seeing, hearing, and smelling. This sensory input, by the mediation of the nerves and other strings and membranes of the body continue to the brain and heart, cause a reaction deemed to be something external. And this reaction is what men call *sense.* It consists of light or color to the eye; to the ear as sound; to the nostril as an odor; to the tongue as a flavor; to the rest of the body as heat, cold, hardness, softness, and other qualities we discern by feeling. All of these qualities are called sensations in the object that caused them.

They are not impressed within us, nor are they anything else but diverse motions, because motion produces nothing but motion. But their appearance to us is an image, whether we are awake or in a dream. And just as pressing, rubbing or striking the eye, makes us imagine a light; pressing the ear produces a noise. In the same way the external bodies we see or hear produce the same impressions by their strong, though unobserved action. For if those colors and sounds were in the objects that cause them, they couldn't be severed from them (as by glasses). In echoes of their reflections we see that they exist. While we know the object we see is in one place, it appears to be elsewhere. And though at a certain distance the real object seems to be the image it creates in us, the object is one thing and the image is another. So, in that sense, everything is nothing but the original image caused by the motion of external things upon our eyes, ears, and other organs.

But the schools of philosophy in all the universities are grounded upon certain texts written by Aristotle, which teach another doctrine, and claim the cause of *vision* is that the thing seen sends out an *apparition;* when the eye receives this, it is called *seeing.* And they claim *hearing* is caused when the thing heard sends out a *noise;* which enters the ear, allowing *hearing.* The cause of *understanding,* they say, is that the thing understood sends out an *intelligible species,* which, coming into the understanding, makes us understand. I'm not saying this to condemn the universities; because I'll write about their function in a commonwealth later. But I must show you which things should be amended in the universities and their doctrines.

From Chapter Two

Of Imagination

When a thing is motionless, it will remain still forever if no one moves it; this is a truth that no one doubts. But when a thing is in motion, the belief that it will move eternally unless someone stops it, according to the reason that nothing can change itself, isn't so easily adopted. Men measure other men and all other things by themselves; and because they find themselves subject to pain after a movement, they think everything else grows tired of motion, and seeks rest; they don't consider other causes. This, according to some schools, is why heavy objects fall down, out of an 'appetite' to rest, and to conserve their nature in a proper place! They absurdly assign knowledge of what is good for their conservation and appetite to inanimate objects!

When a body is once in motion, it will move eternally unless something else hinders it, and whatever hinders it, can't do it in an instant, but over time and by degrees. We see this in waves that roll on in the water long after the wind has ceased. This also happens in man's internal motions, such as dreams. After the object is removed, or the eye shut, we still retain an image of the thing seen, though somewhat more obscure than when we actually look at it. And this is what the Latin language terms *imagination,* from the image made in seeing. This is improperly applied to all the other senses. But the Greeks properly call it *fancy;*

which signifies *appearance*. 'Imagination' is nothing but decaying sense found in men and many other living creatures, whether sleeping or waking.

The decay of sense in waking persons is not the decay of the motion, but an obscuring of it, as when daylight obscures the stars. Due to the amount of input our eyes, ears and other organs receive from external bodies, only dominant impression succeeds. Just as when the light of the sun is dominant, we can't see the stars. In the same way, when any object is removed from our sight, although an impression may remain, other objects work on us, and the imagination of the past object is obscured like a man's voice is obscured by a roaring crowd. The longer we are away from the sight or sense of any object, the weaker the imagination or image in our minds.

In time, the continual change of man's body destroys the parts in which sense took place, so that 'distance of time and place' has the same effect on us. At a great distance what we see appears dim and without distinction; and just as voices grow weak and inarticulate after a great period of time, our imagination or memories of the past grow weak. For example we forget cities we have seen, particular streets and many particular circumstances and actions. This *decaying sense,* if we wish to express the thing itself, we call it *imagination;* but when we wish to express the decay, and signify that the sense is fading, it is called *memory.* Imagination and memory are things, which for diverse considerations have different names.

The memory of many things is called *experience.* Again, imagination refers only to those things that were formerly perceived by sense, either all at once, or in parts. The former, which is the imagining the whole object as it was presented to the sense, is *simple* imagination, such as imagining a man you've never met. The other is *compounded;* for example using the sight of a man at one time, and a horse at another we conceive in our mind a Centaur. When a man compounds the image of himself with the image of the actions of another man, as when a man imagines himself a Hercules or an Alexander the Great, (this often happen to those who read romance novels) it is a compound imagination, and properly considered only a fiction of the mind.

There are also other imaginary things that occur in waking men due to strong sensory impressions. After gazing at the sun, the impression leaves an image on our eyes a long time afterwards. If a man studies geometrical figures too long, and lies awake in the in the dark, he'll see the images of lines and angles before his eyes. But because it's rather uncommon, this kind of illusion has no particular name yet.

The imaginings of those asleep are called *dreams*. And these, like other imaginings, have existed before in part or whole in the senses. And because the brain and nerves are so numb during sleep that they can't be moved by the action of external objects, there can't be any imagination in sleep. There is no new object which can master and obscure them with a more vigorous impression, so a dream must needs be more clear, in this silence of the senses, than our waking thoughts.

And so it comes to pass, that some say it's impossible to distinguish *exactly* between sensory perception and dreaming. If you ask me, when I consider my dreams I don't constantly think of the same persons, places, objects, and actions that I do when awake; nor do I remember so long a train of coherent thoughts when dreaming. I often awake and observe the absurdity of dreams, but never dream of the absurdities of my waking thoughts. I'm well satisfied, that when awake, I know I'm not dreaming, even though when I dream I might think I'm awake.

The most difficult part of separating one's dream from waking thoughts is when by some accident we observe that we haven't slept: which is easy for a person ridden by fear-filled thoughts or whose conscience is very troubled and who slept without getting into bed, for example, someone who nodded off in a chair fully clothed.

And that isn't so rare! The timorous and superstitious, even if perfectly awake, alone in the dark, possessed with fearful tales, are subject to hallucinations and believe they see spirits and ghosts walking in churchyards. But either it's their imagination or a trick by some jester using such superstitious fear and costumes to 'haunt' in the night.

The majority of early pagan religion that worshipped satyrs, fawns, nymphs, and the like (and those who today believe in fairies, ghosts, and goblins, and of the power of witches) arose from this ignorance and inability to distinguish dreams and strong hallucinations from vision and sense. As for witches, I don't think their witchcraft has any real power; but they still should be punished for the false belief that they can perform magic. Their trade is closer to a new religion than a craft or science. And as to fairies and walking ghosts, I think they purposely haven't been debunked simply to keep exorcists and ghost-busters in business.

Nevertheless, I don't doubt that God can create supernatural apparitions and that he does it often, because men need to fear such things more than they fear stagnation or change in nature, but that's no part of the Christian faith. But some evil men do operate under pretext that God can do anything, are they are so bold that they'll say anything that serves their purpose, even if they know it is untrue! A wise man won't believe them even if reason seems to make what they say credible. If this superstitious fear of spirits were taken away, and with it fortune telling from dreams, false prophecies, and many other things that depending upon it, the crafty ambitious persons who abuse simple people would be better citizens than they currently are.

And this should be the task of the universities! Instead they nourish such doctrines! Why? Because they don't know what the imagination or the senses are, nor what they receive nor what they teach us. Some say that hallucinations arise by themselves and have no cause; others, which usually come from the will, and that good thought, is inspired into man by God, and evil thoughts by the Devil. Some teach that good thoughts are poured (infused) into a man by God, and evil ones by the Devil. Some say the senses receive the 'species' of things and deliver them to the common sense and the common sense delivers them to fantasies, and the fantasies to the memory, and the memory to judgment, like the handing of things from one to another! Although they use many words, nothing they say is understood by anyone.

The imagination arises in man, or any other creature with the faculty of imagining, by words or other voluntary signs, this is what we generally call *understanding;* and it is common in man and animal. By habit a dog will recognize the call of his master; and so will many other pets. A form of understanding peculiar to man is understanding not only his will, but his conceptions and thoughts and the conversion of the names of things into affirmations, negations, and other forms of speech. I'll cover this kind of understanding later.

From CHAPTER XIII

The Natural Condition of Mankind

NATURE made men so equal in the faculties of the body and mind that although we find one man sometimes with a stronger body, or with a quicker mind than another, when all is said and done, the difference between men isn't so great that one man can claim exclusive benefits for himself. As to bodily strength, even the weakest has strength enough to kill the strongest, either by trickery or in a pact with others who are also endangered!

Regarding faculties of the mind, very few men have them at all, and then only a limited amount, especially in literary arts and sciences. Why? Because they are born without talent! Yet I still find a greater equality among men in these areas than that in bodily strength. For prudence is simply experience, which equals time, and this is equally bestowed on all men in their undertakings. It is only conceit that makes such equality seem incredible. Almost all men think they are wiser than everyone else, except for a few celebrities that happen to agree with them! That's the nature of men; no matter how many others they are forced to acknowledge as witty or learned; they still won't believe anyone is as wise as they are! Their own wit is in their mind, and other men's wisdom is far away. But this only proves that men are equal rather than unequal. There is no greater proof of equality than the fact that every man is content with his share.

From this 'equality of ability' arises an equality of hope in attaining our ends. And therefore if any two men desire the same thing, which they both can't both have, they become enemies. Sometimes in the pursuit of their own preservation they try to destroy or subdue one another. And so it comes to pass that when an invader doesn't fear another individual; if someone plants, sows, builds, or possess a convenient seat, you may expect that others will probably unite forces to deprive him not only of the fruit of his labor, but also of his life, or liberty. And the invader faces the same danger.

Because of this, there is no way for any man to protect himself. Some take pleasure in dangerous acts of conquest. Others that are at ease within modest bounds can't exist without increasing their power by invasion. Consequently, when such dominion over men is necessary to a man's conservation, it ought to be allowed.

Once again, men have no pleasure, but on the contrary a great deal of grief, in keeping company, where there is no central power over them all. Every man expects that his companions should respect him to the extent he so desires. Any signs of contempt or disrespect will be repaid as far as he dares. As there is no common power to keep them from fighting, they may destroy each other.

So is the nature of man. We find three principal causes of quarrel: competition, diffidence and glory seeking. First, men violate others for riches; second, for safety; and third, for reputation. The first use violence, to make themselves masters of other men's persons, wives, children, and cattle; the second, to defend this theft; the third, for trifles: a word, a smile, a different opinion, and any other sign of disrespect, either directly to them, their family, their friends, their nation, their profession, or their name.

Here we see that during times men live without a common power to keep them in check, they are in that condition called war; a war of every man against the other. For WAR, consists not only of battle, or the act of fighting, but in times where the will to battle is sufficiently known. Therefore the notion of *time*, should be considered in the nature of war; as it is in the nature of weather. The nature of foul weather doesn't lie in a downpour or two; but in many days of rain. So the nature of war doesn't consist of actual fighting; but in the known disposition to do so; during this entire time there isn't any assurance to the contrary. All other times are called PEACE.

In times of war, where every man is the enemy; men live without any security other than their own strength. Under such conditions, there is no place for industry; because profits are uncertain: and consequently no farming; no shipping, no imports; no serious building; no major projects or such things that require great energy; no arts; no letters; no society; and which is worst of all, continual fear, and danger of violent death. The life of man in a state of war is solitary, poor, nasty, brutish, and short.

It may seem strange to someone who hasn't considered these things that nature should render men able to invade and destroy one another. Might he therefore, not trusting my passionate argument, perhaps desire to confirm it by experience? Let him consider that when he takes an adventurous trip he arms himself, and brings comrades; when going to bed, he locks his doors; when even in his house he locks his safe; and this when he knows there are laws, and police officers armed to avenge all crimes against him. What opinion does he have of his fellow citizens, when he drives around armed? Of his fellow citizens, when he locks his doors? Of his children, and employees, when he locks his drawers? Doesn't he accuse mankind by his actions, as I do with my words? But neither of us accuses man's nature. The desires, and other passions of man, are in themselves no sin. Nor are the actions that proceed from those passions, until we know a law that forbids them. Until the laws are made we can't know them: nor can any laws be made until we have agreed on who shall make them.

It may be thought that there were never such times like these or such condition of war. I believe it was never generally so all over the world: but there are many places where they live this way today. The native peoples in many places in America, except the government of small families, in which peace depends on natural lust, have no government at all; and live today in this brutish manner. However it may be perceived, where there is no common power to fear by which men have previously lived under a peaceful government, men degenerate into civil war.

Although there hasn't been a time in which particular men were in a condition of war against one another; still in all ages, kings, and persons of sovereign authority like gladiators with their weapons pointed and their eyes fixed on each another. Their forts, garrisons, and guns are positioned on the frontiers of their kingdoms; and they continually spy upon their neighbors; which is a posture of war. But because they uphold the industry of their subjects by these actions, it doesn't follow that misery accompanies the liberty of particular men.

In this war of every man against every man, it follows that nothing is unjust. The notions of right and wrong, justice and injustice have no place. Where there is no common power, there is no law: where no law, no injustice. Force and fraud are the two cardinal virtues in war. Justice and injustice aren't found in the body or the mind. If they were, they might be in a man alone in the world with his senses and passions. These are qualities that relate to men in society, not in solitude. It also follows in this condition that there is no propriety, no dominion, no *mine* and *yours,* but only 'get what you can' and only for as long as you can hang on to it. And so much for this sick condition in which nature has placed mankind! Luckily, there is a possibility to escape from it, consisting partly in the passions, partly in reason.

What makes men peaceful? Such is the fear of death. The desire for things necessary to live comfortably and the hope to obtain them by work. Reason suggests convenient articles of peace, by which men may cooperate. These articles, called the 'Laws of Nature' follow in the next two chapters.

From CHAPT'ER XIV

On the First and Second Natural Laws and Contracts

THE RIGHT OF NATURE, commonly called 'jus naturale', or natural rights, is the liberty each man has to use his own power as he desires for the preservation of his own nature; that is to say, of his own life, and consequently he is free to do anything he conceives to be the quickest means to his ends.

LIBERTY is understood as the absence of external impediments that may often take away part of a man's power to do what he would like to do; but it can't hinder him from using his remaining powers according to his judgment, and as his reason dictates.

A LAW OF NATURE, 'lex naturale', or natural law, is a general rule discovered through reason, by which a man is forbidden to do whatever is destructive to his life or takes away the means of preserving it. Beyond that he will do whatever he thinks may best preserve it. For although some may confuse jus, and *lex, right* and *law:* yet these things ought to be distinguished. RIGHT consists of the liberty to do, or not to do; whereas LAW binds us to one or the other of them. Law and right differ as much as obligation and liberty; which when taken as one and the same are inconsistent.

Law #1: Seek Peace

The primitive condition of man, as explained earlier, is a condition of war, of one against all. In which case everyone is governed by his own reason; and everything is allowed to help him preserve his life against his enemies. It follows, that in such a condition everyman has a right to everything; even to another's body! And therefore, as long as this natural right of every man to have everything endured, there wasn't enough security for anyone to live out their natural lifespan no matter how wise or strong. Consequently it is a general rule of reason, *that every person, ought to seek peace, as far as realistically possible; and when they can't obtain it, they may use weapons.* The first and fundamental law of nature is: *Seek peace, and follow it.*

Law #2: Self-defense

The second right of nature is, *defend yourself by any means necessary.* From this fundamental law of nature, which commands men to seek peace, we derive this second law; *that a man be willing, when others are also willing, to live and let live.* For as long as every man maintains his right to do anything he likes, all men remain in the condition of war. And if other men won't give up this right to do anything, why should you? To forfeit this right would expose one to attack, rather than create peace, and no one is required to do that. This is the golden rule of the Gospel; *whatsoever you require that others should do to you, that do ye to them.* Do unto others.

I have previously noted the force of words alone is too weak to hold men to the performance of their contracts; but in man's nature there are two imaginable steps to strengthen it. These are either the fear of consequences, or maintaining a reputation. The latter is too rare to be presumed, especially in the pursuit of wealth, rank or sensual pleasure; which constitute the majority of human activity. The most reliable passion is two types of fear; the power of religion or invisible spirits and the power of those persons offended. Of these two, although the former has greater power, the fear of human consequences is commonly the greater fear.

Every man has within him the fear of his own religion, and this has a place in a civil society. The latter doesn't have enough to force men to keep their promises, because in the condition of mere nature because the inequality of power is only known in the event of battle. Before the advent of civil society, or in a war, there is nothing to strengthen a covenant of peace against the temptations of greed, ambition, lust, or other strong desires except the fear of God and the fear of punishment for their sins. Therefore all that can be done to two men not subject to civil power, is to force them to swear by the God he fears: or to take an OATH, *added to* a promise; so that unless he performs his promise he renounces the mercy of his God. Such was the heathen form: "Let Jupiter *kill* me, as I *kill* this beast". Here is our form: "I shall do this and that, so help me *God*". This, with rites and ceremonies used in his religion, greatly increase the fear of breaking the promise.

So it appears that an oath taken any other way is in vain and not an oath: you must swear to God. Men sometimes swear by their kings, out of fear or flattery or to attribute to them a divine honor. Swearing unnecessarily by God profanes his name and swearing by other things is not swearing, but an impious custom of blabbermouths! It appears that the oath adds nothing to the obligation. A lawful contract binds in the sight of God without the oath, as much as with an oath. An unlawful contract is not binding at all even if confirmed by a sworn oath.

From CHAPTER X V

Other Laws of Nature

Law #3: Justice

From this law of nature we are obliged to transfer rights to another. Such unfairly retained rights hinder peace, so there follows a third; that men honor their *covenants:* without which, covenants are in vain, empty words. If people don't keep their promises and honor their contracts, we will remain in a state of war.

In this law of nature we find the fountain and origin of JUSTICE. Prior to forming a contract, no rights were transferred, and every man had a right to everything; consequently, no action was unjust. But when a covenant or contract is made, then to break it is unjust: and this is the definition of INJUSTICE: *not performing a covenant, not honoring your contracts.* And what isn't unjust is just.

But because covenants, or promises of mutual trust, may be accompanied by a fear of non-performance on either part, they are invalid, even though the origin of justice is the making of covenants. Injustice cannot be removed until the fear of breach is eliminated. But while men are in the natural condition of war, this can't be done. Therefore before we can have 'just' and 'unjust' there must be some coercive power to compel men to performance their covenants.

The terror of some punishment, greater than the benefit they expect by breaching their contracts is needed; and there is no such power before the erection of a commonwealth. And this is also gathered out of the ordinary definition of justice in the universities: for they say, that *justice is the constant will of giving to every man his own.* And where there is no *own?* Then there is no propriety, there is no injustice! Where there is no coercive power erected, that is, no commonwealth, there is no propriety and all men have rights to everything. Therefore where there is no commonwealth, there nothing is unjust. The nature of justice consists in keeping valid covenants: but the validity of covenants begins with the constitution of a civil power sufficient to compel men to keep them, which is when propriety begins.

In his heart the fool says there is no such thing as justice; and sometimes also with his tongue. The fool seriously alleges that every man's conservation and contentment is his own concern. There isn't a reason, why every man can't do whatever he likes: and therefore also make, or not make promises; and keep, or not keep contracts when it was to one's benefit.

He doesn't deny there should be covenants; sometimes broken, sometimes kept; and that breaching them may be called injustice, and observing them justice: but the fool questions, whether injustice is so bad, minus the fear of God (which a fool disbelieves) and dictated to his own good, particularly when it creates such a benefit, to put him in a position to disregard the complaints and powers of other men.

The words 'just' and 'unjust' when attributed to men signify one thing; and another thing when attributed to actions. When they are attributed to men, they signify the conformity or inconformity of manners to reason. But when attributed to actions, they signify conformity or non-conformity to reason of particular actions. A just man takes great care that all his actions are just. An unjust man neglects this care.

Such men are often called 'righteous' and 'unrighteous' than 'just' and 'unjust'; though they mean the same thing. Therefore a righteous man doesn't lose the title of 'just' by one, or even a few unjust actions that proceed from a sudden passion or mistake. Nor does an unrighteous man lose his 'unjust' character for actions he does or doesn't do out of fear: because his will isn't framed by justice, but by the apparent benefit of consequences. What gives human actions the relish of justice, is a certain rare nobility or courage by which a man scorns fraud and broken promises. This type of justice is what is meant when justice is called a virtue and injustice a vice.

But just actions denominate men, not justness, but *guiltlessness:* and injustice the same way, which is called injury, we call them *guilty.* Again, the injustice of manners is the intention or aptitude to do injury, and is unjust even before one proceeds to act, even before any individual person is injured. But the injustice of an action, that is to say injury, supposes an injured person; namely him, to whom the covenant was made: and therefore often the injury was received by one man, when the damage done to another.

Law # 4: Gratitude

Just as justice depends on an antecedent covenant; gratitude depends on antecedent grace; that is, to an antecedent free gift. The fourth law of nature may be conceived in this form, *that a man who receives a benefit from another's kindness, should be certain whomever gives it, has no reason to regret this act of goodwill.* Every man gives with intention of bringing good things to himself; and because gift is voluntary, the object is his own good. If men see this frustrated, there will be no benevolence, trust or mutual help; no reconciliation. Therefore they remain in the condition of *war;* which is contrary to the first and fundamental law of nature, to *seek peace.* The breach of this law is called *ingratitude;* and has the same relation to grace that injustice has to obligation by covenant.

Law #5: Accommodation or Against Greed.

A fifth law of nature is accommodation or complaisance; *that every man should strive to accommodate himself to the rest.* To understand this we may consider, that in men's aptness to society, a diverse natures arises from diverse affections; not unlike stones brought together for building of an edifice. For just as that irregular stone takes more room from others than it fills; it thereby hinders the building, is thrown away by the builders. So, too will a greedy man retain things that are superfluous to him, but necessary to others. If this stubbornness can't be corrected, he should be cast out of society as cumbersome. For every man, by right and by necessity of nature, is supposed to try his best to obtain necessities for his conservation. If someone opposes another's necessities for his own superfluous greed is guilty of the war that will follow, which is contrary to the fundamental law of nature, *to seek peace.* The observers of this law, may be called sociable, those contrary to this law are called, *stubborn, anti-social, greedy and intractable.*

Law #6: Pardon

A sixth law of nature is *that after considering the future, a man ought to pardon the past offences of those that truly repent.* For pardoning is nothing but granting peace. However when granted to those that persevere in their hostility, it's not peace, but fear; yet when not granted to those who will be cautious in the future, is sign of an aversion to peace; and therefore contrary to the law of nature.

Law #7: No Revenge

A seventh law is that when considering *revenge*, or retribution of evil for evil, *men shouldn't look at the severity of the evil done, but towards the greatness of the good to follow.* We shouldn't inflict punishment with any other reason than the correction of the offender, or the instruction of others. For this law is consequent with the previous law that commanded pardon, based upon the security of a better future. Besides, revenge without setting an example or to improve the future is simply enjoying the pain of another with no purpose in mind, and this is vain and contrary to reason. To hurt without reason invites the introduction of war; which is against the law of nature; and is commonly called *cruelty.*

Law #8: Against Hate

All signs of hatred and contempt provoke fighting. Unfortunately, most men would rather risk their life for revenge. Thus, we may set down as an eight law of nature: *That no man by deed, word, countenance, or gesture, declare hatred, or contempt of another.* The breach of this law is commonly called *contumely.*

Law #9: Against Pride

The question of 'who is the better man' has no place in nature where all men are generally equal. The inequality we now face has been introduced by civil laws. I know that in the first book of his *Politics,* Aristotle made some men more worthy to command by nature, (that is, the wiser sort, philosophers such as himself) and some men servile by nature, meaning those that had strong bodies, (but not philosophers). As if master and servant were not introduced by consent of men, but by difference of wit! This is not only against reason; but also against experience. There are very few so foolish, that would rather be governed by anyone other than themselves! Seldom do the wise get the upper hand over those who trust their own wisdom. If nature made men equal, that equality should acknowledged. If nature made men unequal; but men still consider themselves equal, and won't enter into conditions of peace except upon equal terms, well, then such equality must be admitted. Therefore the ninth law of nature is, *that every man acknowledges others as his equals by nature.* The breach of this law is called *pride.*

Law #10: Against Arrogance

This law depends on another, *that upon entry into conditions of peace, no man may reserve for himself any right that he won't reserve for everyone else.* It's necessary that all men seek peace and lay down certain rights of nature, because is it necessary to retain some liberties such as right to govern their own bodies, to enjoy air, water, motion, travel from place to place, and all those other things, without which a man can't live, or can't live well. In this case, in making peace, men can't demand for themselves what they won't grant to others. Such actions are contrary to the preceding law that commands the acknowledgment of natural equality. We call those who observer this law *modest,* and the breakers of it we call *arrogant.* The Greeks call the violation of this law 'a desire for more than a fair share'.

Law #11: Equity

Also if *a man is entrusted to judge men in disputes,* it is a precept of natural law, *that he deals with them equally.* For without this, the controversies of men can only be determined by war. If he is partial in his judgments, he will deter men from using judges and arbitrators; and consequently, violate a fundamental natural law and cause war. The observance of this law of equal distribution using his reason is called 'equity' or distributive justice: the violation, favoritism or *exception of persons.*

Law #12: Equal Common Use

And from this followed another law, *that things that can't be divided must be enjoyed in common, if possible; and if the quantity of the thing permits it, without restraint; otherwise, proportionally to the number of those who have rights to it.* Otherwise the distribution is unequal, and contrary to equity.

Law #13: Use of Lottery

But some things can't be divided or enjoyed in common. Then, the laws of nature which prescribe equity require *that the entire right; or alternate use, or first possession, be determined by lot.* For equal distribution is one of the laws of nature; and in some cases no other means of equal distribution can be imagined, except drawing lots.

Law #14: First Seizure

Of lots there be two sorts, *arbitrary,* and *natural.* Arbitrary, is that which is agreed on by the competitors: natural, is either *primogeniture,* which the Greeks call *"given by lot"* or *"first seizure".* And therefore those things which cannot be enjoyed in common, nor divided, ought to be adjudged to the first possessor; and in some cases to the first born, or as acquired by lot.

Law # 15: Mediation and Safe Conduct

It is also a law of nature, *that all men that mediate peace be allowed safe conduct.* For the law that commanded peace as the *end,* commanded intercession as the *means;* and to intercession that means is the safe conduct of mediators, arbitrators and judges.

Law #16: Arbitration

Although men may be willing to observe these laws, nevertheless questions may arise concerning a man's action; first, whether it was done, or not done; secondly, if done, was it was against the law? Or not against the law? The former is called a question *of fact;* the latter a question *of right.* Therefore, unless the parties in question mutually agree to abide by judgment *of* a third, they are as far from peace as when they started. This third party to whose sentence they submit is called an 'arbitrator'. Therefore it is a law of nature, *that those at controversy must submit to the final judgment of an arbitrator.*

Law #17: Independent Judges

Seeing that every man presumably does everything for his own benefit, no man is a fit arbitrator or judge of his own case. Even if he were fit, equity must allow each party equal benefits; therefore if one party in the dispute can be admitted as a judge, so can the other. In the end this would just continue the controversy and the cause of war, and this is contrary to the laws of nature.

Law #18: Impartial Judges

For the same reason no man ought to be the arbitrator in any case where greater profit or honor, or pleasure apparently arises out of the victory of one party, rather than the other. If so, he has taken a bribe and no man can be obliged to trust him. And this too is a controversy, and the condition of war remains, contrary to the laws of nature.

Law #19: Witnesses

And in a controversy of *fact* if the judge can't credit one side more than another, and if there are no other arguments, the judge must give credit to a third person; or to a third and fourth, or even more witnesses. Otherwise the question is undecided, and left to be settled by force, which is contrary to the laws of nature.

Summary

These are the laws of nature dictating peace and a means of conserving of men in multitudes; and these laws comprise the doctrine of a civil society. There are other things related to the destruction of particular men; such as drunkenness, and all other forms of intemperance; and these may also be added to those things forbidden by laws of nature; but they don't need to be mentioned at this time.

This may seem too subtle a deduction of natural law to be noticed by most men, who are usually too busy getting food. The rest are too negligent to understand; yet to end any excuses, they have been condensed into one easy law, intelligible to all: *Don't do to another, which you wouldn't like done to yourself.* This shows that if we do nothing in learning the laws of nature except weighing other men's actions against our own, they seem too heavy to put into the other part of the balance. Our own passions and self-love may add nothing to the weight; and then all the laws of nature will appear very reasonable.

The laws of nature oblige or bind one to a desire that *should* take place: but not always a desire they *must* put into action. One *should* be modest and keep all their promises in a time and place as is fitting, but must not keep them where no other man would do so. That would only make him a victim and procure his own certain ruin, which is contrary to the ground rules of nature, which tend to preserve. And again, if he is sufficiently sure that others will follow the same laws towards him, but if he refuses to follow them himself, he is not a peace seeker, but a warmonger; and consequently he invites his destruction by violence.

And whatever law binds with *should,* might be broken by a fact contrary to the law or by a fact in accord with it, in case one thinks differently. For although his action is in accord with the law; his purpose may be against the law where the obligation is a *must,* then there is a breach. The laws of nature are immutable and eternal; for injustice, ingratitude, arrogance, pride, iniquity, acception of persons, and the rest, can never be made lawful. It can never be that war shall preserve life, and peace destroy it. The same laws, because they serve a desire or a constant endeavor, are easy to observe. For they require nothing but an attempt, that one try to perform and fulfill them; and one that follows the law is just.

And their science is the only true moral philosophy. For moral philosophy is nothing other than the science of what is *good* and *evil,* in the conversation and in the society of mankind. *Good* and *evil* are names that signify our appetites and aversions; which in the different cultures, customs, and doctrines of men, are different. Men differ not only in their judgment of what is pleasant and unpleasant to senses, but also on what is conformable or disagreeable to reason in the activities of daily life. No! The same man, in different times even differs from himself. One day he praises something as good, the next day he curses it and calls it evil; thus arise disputes, controversies, and finally wars. And therefore, as long as a man lives in the condition of primitive nature, which is a condition of war, private appetites are the measure of good and evil. We all agree on this: peace is good, and therefore the way toward peace is good. As I have shown they are *justice, gratitude, modesty, equity, mercy,* and the rest of the laws of nature. They are *moral virtues* and their contraries *vices,* are evil.

The science of virtue and vice is moral philosophy, and the true doctrine of the laws of nature is the true moral philosophy. But the writers of moral philosophy, though they acknowledge the same virtues and vices, don't see the source of their goodness. Nor should virtues be praised as the means of peaceable, sociable, and comfortable living, which places them in a mediocrity of passions. Does the degree of daring, but not the cause, make courage? Or the quantity of a gift, but not the cause, make generosity?

These dictates of reason, which men used to improperly call laws, are only conclusions or theorems concerning conduct related to self-conservation and self-defense. Whereas proper law is the right to command others. But if we consider the same theorems as delivered in the word of God, who commands all things; they are properly called laws.

—Thomas Hobbes

Commentary on Hobbes Law's

Was Hobbes an Atheist? To many of his contemporary readers he certainly met their definition of one: he argued that everything is simple materialism or 'bodies in motion'. He also derided superstitious practices in both the Catholic and Protestant churches and created a powerful argument against the 'Divine Right of Kings' by asserting that 'All civil authority is derived originally from the people'. He found oaths in the name of God almost worthless. His friends in the scientific world were birds of a feather. The evidence may lead us in that direction, but his actions leave room for doubt.

It is difficult to sum up Hobbes in a sentence, but I will attempt to do so. He was a monarchist in his heart, a scientist in his head and a skeptic in his soul.

PART II
LOCKE

A Short Biography of John Locke (August 29,1632. Died October 28,1704.)

John Locke was born into a solid Puritan background. He was educated by his father, a captain in the parliamentary army, a lawyer by profession and a small landowner. Young Locke won a scholarship to Christ Church, Oxford and faced the same discontent described by Hobbes. Unimpressed by the 'peripatetic' or 'walking school' of the Greek Philosopher Aristotle then in vogue at Oxford, Locke half-heartedly finished his bachelor's and master's degree and began to lecture for the university. Like Hobbes, he became interested in science, especially medicine, which he practiced in that gentlemanly way of the times, without obtaining a doctorate.

This later served as a doorway to his new passion; politics. After serving on a diplomatic mission to Germany, he left Oxford to enter the wild political landscape of London. A chance meeting led him to become the physician and general confidant of Lord Ashley, then Chancellor of the Exchequer and soon to be the first Earl of Shaftesbury. He and Hobbes had a mutual friend in the scientist, Robert Boyle. In 1668 Locke was elected Fellow of the Royal Society, an honor that escaped Hobbes. After Boyle's death, Locke edited one of his works on air. Science and politics were Locke's lifeblood.

But politics are fickle; and when Shaftesbury fell from grace in 1675, so did Locke. Locke, again like Hobbes, went into French exile and worked on his *Essay on Human Understanding*. After four years, Earl Shaftesbury rose to power, but his comeback ended in 1681 when his plots against the King led to a charge of treason and exile in Holland, where he died. Afraid he too might be arrested, Locke fled to Holland as "Dr. Van der Linden" where he continued work on the Essay and may have played a part in the Glorious Revolution of 1688. He returned to England in the entourage of the future Queen, Princess Mary and was appointed to various governmental posts, but continued writing and corresponding with his many friends, such as Sir Issac Newton.

Despite flattering insistence by the King personally, poor health caused Locke to decline several important Royal posts. John Locke spent his last years in biblical studies, especially St. Paul's Epistles. He was buried at High Laver Church near Oates, England.

Selections from "An Essay Concerning Human Understanding" by John Locke, Updated, Edited and Modernized by Prof. Les Sutter (copyright of paraphrase, 2003)

AN ESSAY CONCERNING HUMAN

UNDERSTANDING (abridged)

INTRODUCTION

This is an inquiry into understanding what is pleasant and useful. Since understanding sets man above the rest of beings, and gives him all the advantages and dominion he has over them, it's certainly a subject worth looking into. Understanding, like the eye, makes us see and perceive all other things, but takes no notice of itself. It requires exertion to see understanding from a distance, as its own object. But whatever difficulties lie in the way of this inquiry; whatever keeps us in the dark about ourselves, I'm sure that any light we can throw on the subject about our own understanding will be very pleasant, and yield us great advantages in directing our thoughts while we search for other things.

Design.—This is my purpose: to inquire into the originality, certainty and extent of *human knowledge,* together with the grounds and degrees of *belief, opinion,* and *assent.* At present I won't meddle with the physical mind or examine its essence; nor about how our bodies arrive at sensations using our organs. Nor about *ideas* in our understandings; and whether the formation of those ideas depend on matter or not. Although these speculations are entertaining I decline to handle them because they digress from my current project.

It's enough that my purpose considers the discriminating faculties of a man applied to common objects. I imagine I haven't totally wasted my time if I can give account for the ways in which our understanding attains the notions of things we have. Perhaps I can also set down some measures of our certainty for our knowledge; or the grounds of persuasions found among men, all so different and contradictory; and yet asserted somewhere or other with such assurance and confidence! If one views the contrary opinions of mankind and yet observes at the same time how fondly they are embraced and resolutely maintained, one may suspect that either there is no truth, or that mankind can't attain certain knowledge of it.

Method.—It is therefore worthwhile to mark the boundaries between opinion and knowledge and examine how we measure uncertain knowledge. We ought to regulate our assent and moderate our persuasion. In order to do so I will pursue the following methods.

First, I will look into the original ideas a man observes, and is conscious of in his own mind, and the ways in which understanding of them takes place.

Secondly, I shall attempt to show what *knowledge* our understanding has of those ideas and the certainty, evidence, and extent of it.

Third, I will look into the nature and grounds of *faith* or *opinion:* I mean our assent to any proposition considered true, but of whose truth we have no certain knowledge. And here we will examine the reasons and degrees of assent.

What does an idea stand for? Before I proceed to my thoughts on this subject, at the start I must ask the reader to pardon my frequent use of the word *idea* which they will find in the following treatise. This term best stands for whatever may be the *object* of understanding when a man thinks. I have used it to express whatever is meant by *phantasm, notion, species,* or whatever it is the mind is employed in thinking about; and I couldn't avoid using it frequently.

I presume you can easily grant me that such ideas exist in men's minds: everyone is conscious of them in themselves; and your own words and actions should satisfy you that they are in others minds too.

BOOK I

NEITHER PRINCIPLES NOR IDEAS ARE INNATE

Chapter I

AGAINST INNATE SPECULATIVE PRINCIPLES

Why our path to knowledge is not innate.—It's an established opinion among some that understanding contains certain *innate principles;* some primary notions, stamped on the mind of man, received by the soul at its very first beginning. It would be sufficient to convince unprejudiced readers of the falseness of this supposition, if I show how men barely using their natural faculties, may attain all the knowledge they have without the help of any innate impressions and arrive at certainty without any original notions. I imagine it's impertinent to suppose colors are innate ideas, as is the power to receive them by the eyes from external objects. It is unreasonable to attribute truths to innate characters when we have faculties allowing easy and certain knowledge of them as if they were originally imprinted on the mind.

Because a man isn't permitted to follow his own thoughts in the search of truth without censure when they lead him off the beaten path, I'll give the reasons that made me doubt, in case I am in error. I'll leave them for consideration by those of us ready to embrace truth wherever we find it.

General Assent the Great Argument.—There is nothing more taken for granted than certain principles, both speculative and practical, agreed upon by all mankind: which they therefore argue, must be impressions received at birth and brought into the world like any of their inherent faculties. Universal consent does not prove something is innate. The argument drawn from universal consent is unfortunate because if there were certain truths all agreed upon, it wouldn't prove them innate, especially if another way can be shown how men arrive at universal agreement, which I presume may be done.

'What is, is.' and 'It is impossible for something to be, and, at the same time, not to be.' are not universally assented to. But, which is worse? This argument of universal consent used to 'prove' innate principles seems to me a demonstration that there aren't any. There aren't any principles that mankind grants universal assent.

I'll begin with the speculative statements above because they have such a reputation that is seems strange to question them. But these propositions are far from having universal assent, because a great part of mankind doesn't even know them.

They aren't naturally imprinted on the mind because children, idiots, etc. have no apprehension of them. This is enough to destroy that 'universal assent' necessary to all innate truths. It seems nearly a contradiction to say that there are truths imprinted on the soul, which it perceives or doesn't understand: imprinting, if it signifies anything, is nothing else but making certain truths perceivable.

To imprint anything on the mind without the mind's perceiving it seems to me hardly intelligible! If children and idiots have souls and minds with those impressions upon them, they must unavoidably perceive them, and necessarily know and agree to these truths, and since they don't it's evident there are no such impressions. For if they aren't naturally imprinted, how can they be innate? And if they are imprinted, how can they be unknown? To say a notion is imprinted on the mind, and yet at the same time to say, that the mind is ignorant of it, and never yet took notice of it, is to make this impression nothing.

No proposition can be said to be 'in the mind' which it never knew or of which it was never conscious. Using the same reasoning, all the propositions the mind is capable of assenting to be imprinted and true. If one can be in the mind, (which it never yet knew) it must be—only because it is capable of knowing it! And so the mind has all the truths it might ever know! No! Truths may be imprinted on the mind which it never knew, nor ever shall know, and a man may live a long time and die in ignorance of many truths of which his mind was capable of knowing, and that's certain!

If the capacity of 'knowing' is the natural impression, all the truths a man ever comes to know will all be innate. This whole point amounts to nothing but improper speech; while it pretends to assert the contrary, it says nothing different from those who deny innate principles. For no one ever denied the mind was capable of knowing several truths. The capacity, they say, is innate; the knowledge acquired. But then, why look to certain innate maxims? If truths can be imprinted on the mind without being perceived, I see no difference between any truth the mind is *capable* of knowing in respect to the original. They must all be innate or otherwise, it's impossible to distinguish them. Therefore whoever talks of 'innate notions' can't mean any distinct truths it never perceived and is wholly ignorant of. So, to be in the understanding, and not to be understood; to be in the mind and never to be perceived, is all one as to say 'anything is and is not in the mind or understanding'!

If therefore these two propositions, 'What is, is,' and 'It is impossible to be and not to be,' are naturally imprinted children can't be ignorant of them: infants, and all that have souls, must necessarily have them in their understandings, know the truth of them, and assent to it. And they don't.

BOOK Il

OF IDEAS

Chapter I

OF IDEAS IN GENERAL, AND THEIR ORIGINAL

Idea: The Object of Thinking.—Every man is conscious that he thinks and his mind is applied by thinking about *ideas*. It's past doubt that men have several ideas in their minds such as *whiteness, hardness, sweetness, thinking, motion, man, elephant, army, drunkenness,* and others. How does he obtain them?
I know it's a popular doctrine that men have native ideas and original characters stamped on their minds at birth. I have already examined this idea in general and I suppose what I've said is easier to accept when I've shown where understanding may get it's ideas, by which ways and degrees they may come into the mind. I shall appeal to every one's own observation and experience.

Why is the mind is a tabula rasa, or blank slate?

All Ideas come from Sensation or Reflection. Let's suppose the mind is a piece of white paper, void of all characters, without any ideas: How is it furnished? Where does it obtain that vast store of boundless imagination man has painted on it with an almost endless variety? Where did it obtain all the materials of reason and knowledge? To this I answer, in one word, EXPERIENCE. All our knowledge is founded and ultimately derives itself from our observation of external objects, or from the internal operations of our mind's perception and reflection. This supplies our understanding with all the materials of thinking. These two are the fountains of knowledge; from these spring ALL the ideas we have.

The Objects of Sensation and Source of Ideas. First, our senses convey several distinct perceptions of things to the mind; according to the various ways those objects affect them. Those *ideas* we have of *yellow, white, heat, cold, soft, hard, bitter, sweet,* and all those things we call sensible qualities, produce those perceptions when conveyed from external objects into the mind. This great source of most of our ideas depends wholly upon our senses, and sends them to our 'understanding'. I call our senses and understanding, 'sensation'.

The Operations of our minds and their source. Secondly, the other fountain from which experience furnishes the understanding with ideas is the perception of the operations of our own mind within us, as it is employed on ideas. These furnish the understanding with another set of ideas, which couldn't be obtained externally. Examples are perception, thinking, doubting, believing, reasoning, knowing, willing and all the different actions of our minds. We use self-observation to receive these into our understanding of distinct ideas, just as we do from objects affecting our senses. This source of ideas is wholly internal and has nothing to do with external objects (although very much like it) and might be called 'internal sense'. I call the other 'sensation', so I'll call this REFLECTION, or the ideas the mind gets by reflecting on its own operations. By reflection I mean when the mind takes notice of its own operations, their manner and why there are ideas of these operations in the understanding. These two external, material things, objects of SENSATION and the operations of our mind, are the objects of REFLECTION, the original place where all of our ideas begin. I use the term 'operations' here in a wider sense, not as comprehending the mind's actions about its ideas, but as some sort of passion sometimes arising from them, such as 'satisfaction' or 'uneasiness' arising from any thought.

All our ideas arise from one of these. I believe 'understanding' doesn't seem to have the faintest idea about any ideas it didn't receive from these two. External objects furnish the mind with the ideas of sensible qualities, which are all those different perceptions they produce in us; and the mind furnishes 'understanding' with ideas of its own operations.

In these, and their several combinations, we'll find our whole stock of ideas; we have nothing in our minds which didn't arrive in one of these two ways. Let anyone examine his own thoughts, thoroughly search into his understanding; and then tell me if all his original ideas are anything other than the objects of his senses, or of the operations of his mind, as objects of his reflection. And however much knowledge he imagines to have, he will see that his ideas are only imprinted by these two. Although some are compounded by understanding, as we'll see later.

Does the soul exist antecedent to the beginnings of life in the body? I'll leave that open to dispute. We know certainly, by experience, that we *sometimes* think; and then draw the infallible conclusion that there is something in us that has a power to think. But whether that substance *perpetually* thinks or not, we can only know what experience reports to us. To say that actual thinking is essential to the soul and inseparable from it is to beg the question, and not to prove it by reason; which is necessary, as it isn't a self-evident proposition. But is, 'the soul always thinks,' a self-evident proposition that everybody agrees to at first hearing? I'll leave it up to you. It's doubtful whether I thought at all last night.

The question offers as proof a hypothesis which is the very thing in dispute! One may thus prove anything: suppose that all ticking watches think, and suddenly it is sufficiently proved, and beyond doubt that my ticking watch thought all last night! But one ought to build his hypothesis on facts, and build it from sensory experience, and not presume on facts in favor of the hypothesis, (that is, because he supposes it to be so). This way of proving amounts to this: that I must necessarily think all last night, because another supposes I always think, though I myself cannot perceive that I always do so.

But men in love with their opinions not only suppose what is in question, but also allege wrong facts. How else could anyone make it an inference of mine that a thing is not, because we are not sensible of it in our sleep? I didn't say there isn't a soul in a man, because he is not sensible of it in his sleep; but I do say, he cannot *think* at any time, waking or sleeping, without being sensible of it. Our being sensible of it isn't necessary to anything but to our thoughts; and to them it is necessary; and to them it always will be necessary, until we can think without being conscious of it.

Chapter II

SIMPLE IDEAS

Uncompounded Appearances.

To better understand the nature, manner, and extent of our knowledge, one thing needs to be carefully observed concerning the ideas we have; and that is, that some of them are simple and some complex.

Although the qualities that affect our senses are so united and blended, there is no separation, no distance between them. Yet it's plain the ideas they produce in the mind enter by the senses simple and unmixed. For, although sight and touch often take in information from the same object, at the same time, different ideas are produced. A man may see motion and color at the same time. The hand might feel softness and warmth in the same piece of wax. Still, simple ideas united in the same subject are just as perfectly distinct as those that come in by different senses. The coldness and hardness which a man feels in a piece of ice are distinct ideas in the mind, just as the smell and whiteness of a lily; or as the taste of sugar, and smell of a rose. And there is nothing plainer to a man than the clear and distinct perception he has of those simple ideas; which, being uncompounded, contains nothing in it but one uniform appearance, or conception in the mind, and is not distinguishable into different ideas.

Furthermore, the mind can't make or destroy them. These simple ideas, the materials of all our knowledge, are suggested to the mind only by sensation and reflection. When the understanding is filled with these simple ideas, it has the power to repeat, compare, and unite them almost to infinity and make new, complex ideas. But it's not even the quickest thinker has the power to invent one new simple idea in the mind, nor can any force of the understanding destroy those that exist. Man's little world of understanding is much the same as it is in the great world of visible things. His power, however managed, reaches no farther than to compound and divide. We cannot make a new particle of matter, or destroy one atom of what is already in being. Everyone will discover the same inability in themselves. Simply attempt to create a simple idea not received in by the senses from external objects, or by reflection from the operations of the mind. Try to create a new taste or a new scent the tongue and nose don't know: and when you can do this, I will conclude a blind man knows colors or that a deaf man knows true and distinct sounds.

Chapter III

OF SIMPLE IDEAS OF SENSE

Division of Simple Ideas. To better conceive the ideas we receive from sensation, we should consider them in reference to the different ways they approach our minds and make themselves perceivable. First, there are some which come into our minds by one sense only. Secondly, there are others that enter the mind by more than one sense. Others come only from reflection. Finally, there are some that make themselves known to the mind by *all means of sensation and reflection.* We shall consider them separately.

Ideas from one Sense. Some ideas have gained admittance through one sense, which is peculiarly adapted to receive them. Thus light and colors, such as red, yellow, blue, with their several shades and mixtures, such as green, scarlet, purple, sea-green, and the rest, only enter through the eyes. All kinds of noises, sounds, and tones, only by the ears. Tastes and smells by the nose and palate. And if these organs, or the nerves which convey them to the brain, are dysfunctional, they have no other way to bring themselves into the mind and be perceived by the understanding.

OF SIMPLE IDEAS OF REFLECTION

Simple ideas are the operations of mind about its other ideas. The mind receives ideas externally. It may also turn inward and observe its own actions about ideas it has and then have other ideas capable of being the object of contemplation, just like any of those it received from foreign things. The ideas of perception and willing arise from reflection. The two great and principal actions of the mind are: perception, or thinking; and volition, or willing. The power of thinking is called the 'understanding', and the power of volition is called the 'will' and these two abilities in the mind are denominating faculties.

OF FAITH AND REASON, AND THEIR DISTINCT PROVINCES

It's necessary to know their boundaries. As shown above, 1. We are of necessity ignorant, and want all sorts of knowledge and ideas. 2. We are ignorant and want rational knowledge and proofs. 3. We want certain knowledge and clearly determined specific ideas. 4. We want probability to direct us in matters where we have neither knowledge of our own nor the testimony of other men to base our reason upon.

Thus premised, I think we may lay down *the boundaries between faith and reason:* the lack of which has been the cause of great disorders, great disputes, and mistakes in the world. Until it has been resolved how far reason and faith may guide us, we will argue in vain, and try to convert one another in matters of religion.

Faith and Reason Distinguished. I find every sect will gladly use reason as far as it helps them, and where it fails them, they cry out, "It is matter of faith, and above reason!" And I don't see how they can argue with anyone, or ever convince anyone who makes use of the same plea, without setting down strict boundaries between faith and reason. This ought to be the first point established in all questions about faith. *Reason* as distinguished from *faith,* is the discovery of the certainty or probability of such propositions or truths, which the mind arrives at by deduction made from such ideas, obtained by its natural faculties (sensation or reflection). *Faith* is the assent to any proposition, not obtained by the deductions of reason, but upon crediting a proposal as coming from God by some extraordinary way of communication. This we call *revelation.*

No new simple Idea can be conveyed by traditional Revelation. I say that no man inspired by God can by any revelation communicate to others any new simple ideas which they didn't have before from sensation or reflection. Whatever impressions he himself may have had from God, if new simple ideas, cannot be conveyed to another, either by words or any other signs. Why? Because words, by their immediate operation on us, cause no other ideas but their natural sounds: and the custom of using them as signs excites and revives latent ideas; but only ideas that were there before. Words, seen or heard, only recall thoughts of those ideas they were signs of, but they can't introduce any perfectly new, and formerly unknown simple ideas. The same holds true of all other signs; they can't signify things of which we never had any idea.

Thus whatever things St. Paul discovered when he was swept up into heaven; whatever new ideas his mind received, all the description, etc. we can only say, "There are such things as eye has not seen, nor ear heard, nor has it entered into the heart of man to conceive." Supposing God should supernaturally show anyone a species of creatures inhabiting Jupiter or Saturn which has six senses; and imprint on his mind the ideas conveyed by a sixth sense: using words he couldn't reproduce in other men the ideas imprinted by that sixth sense. None of us could convey the idea of any color, by the sound of words, into a blind man having the other four senses. Our simple ideas are the foundation, and sole matter of all our notions and knowledge. We must depend wholly on our reason, our natural faculties; and we can't receive them from traditional revelation. I say, *traditional revelation,* in distinction to *original revelation.* By the one, I mean that first impression which is made immediately by God on the mind of any man, to which we cannot set any bounds; and by the other, those impressions delivered over to others in words, and the ordinary ways of conveying our conceptions one to another.

Secondly, traditional revelation may make us know propositions also knowable by reason, but without the same certainty that reason does. The same truths discovered and conveyed from revelation are discoverable by reason, and by those ideas we may have naturally. So God might, by revelation, discover the truth of any proposition in Euclid; and men, by the natural use of their faculties, may make the discovery themselves. In these things there is little need of revelation, because God furnished us with natural and surer means to arrive at this knowledge.

Whatever truth we discovery, the knowledge and contemplation of our own ideas will always be more certain than those conveyed by *traditional revelation.* The knowledge we have that this revelation came first from God can never be as sure as the knowledge we have from the clear and distinct perception of the agreement or disagreement of our own ideas. If it were revealed some ages ago that the three angles of a triangle were equal to two right ones, I might agree to the truth of that proposition, upon the credit of the tradition, that it was revealed. Yet, that would never amount to as great a certainty as the knowledge of it by comparing and measuring the two right angles and the three angles of a triangle.

The same is true in matters-of-fact knowable through our senses. The history of the flood is conveyed to us by writings that were originally revelation, yet no one will say he has knowledge of the flood as clear and certain as Noah, unless he himself would have been alive and seen it. He has no greater an assurance than his senses. Perhaps because it is written in the book Moses inspired? He can't be sure that Moses wrote that book unless he saw Moses writing it. The assurance of its being a revelation is less still than the assurance of his senses.

Even Original Revelation can't be admitted against the clear Evidence of Reason. In propositions whose certainty is built upon the clear perception of the agreement or disagreement of our ideas, by immediate intuition in self-evident propositions, or by evident deductions of reason in demonstrations, we don't need the assistance of revelation. The natural ways of knowledge could settle them, or has done so already. This is the greatest assurance we can possibly have of anything, unless God immediately reveals it to us. Even then our assurance that it's a revelation from God isn't greater than our knowledge. Nothing can overrule plain knowledge or rationally persuade any man to admit something to be true which directly contradicts the clear evidence of his own understanding.

Since no evidence of such revelations can exceed the certainty of our intuitive knowledge, we can never receive anything as truth that is directly contrary to our clear and distinct knowledge. The ideas of 'one body at one place' clearly agree, and the mind has such an evident perception of this that we can never agree to a proposition that affirms the 'same body to be in two distant places at once', even on the authority of a 'divine revelation'. We consider it impossible for the same body to be in two places at once. And therefore no proposition can be considered 'divine revelation' if it is contradictory to our clear, intuitive knowledge.

If doubtful propositions take the place of self-evident ones, this would subvert the principles and foundations of all knowledge and evidence and there would be no difference between truth and falsehood, no measures of credible and incredible. What we know for certain will give way to what may possibly be mistaken. In propositions contrary to clear perception, it will futile to endorse them as matters of faith. They can't gain our approval under 'faith' or any other title whatsoever. For faith can never convince us of anything that contradicts our knowledge. Even though faith is founded on the testimony of God (who cannot lie) we can't be sure it is a divine revelation beyond our own knowledge.

The whole strength of certainty depends upon our knowledge that God revealed it; and in the case where the proposition supposedly revealed contradicts our knowledge or reason, will always have the following objection: we can't tell how to conceive whatever comes from God if it overturns all the principles of knowledge he has given us. This renders all our faculties useless and destroys the most excellent part of his workmanship, our understanding; and puts us in a condition where we have less light than a beast that perishes. For if the mind of man can never have clear evidence of anything of 'divine revelation', as it does of the principles of its own reason, it can never have a basis to desert reason for revelation.

Traditional Revelation. A man needs reason even in immediate, original revelation. But all those who didn't have an immediate revelation, but instead receive them through writings or word of mouth, well, reason has a greater role, and is the only thing that can induce us to believe them. Those matters-of-faith which are purely 'divine revelation' and nothing else, called 'faith' are only connected to propositions that are supposed to be divinely revealed. So I don't see how those who make revelation alone the sole object of faith can say, "this is a matter of faith, and not of reason", and believe this or that proposition was divine inspiration, unless that proposition or book was communicated by divine inspiration. Without such a revelation, the believing or not believing of divine authority can never be matter of faith, but matter of reason. I must use my reason, which can never require me to believe anything contrary to it. It is impossible for reason to procure agree with what it finds unreasonable.

In all things where we have clear evidence from our ideas, reason is the proper judge. Although revelation may consent with it, confirm its dictates, it cannot invalidate its decrees, nor can we be obliged to abandon it under a pretence that it is 'a matter of faith' when we have clear and evident reason that it is true. Faith has no authority against the plain and clear dictates of reason.

Since a man can never have certain knowledge that a proposition which contradicts the clear principles of his knowledge was divinely revealed, he is bound to consider it a matter of reason, and not swallow it, without examination, as a matter of faith.

All propositions which the mind can judge from naturally acquired ideas are matters of reason. Whatever God has revealed is certainly true: no doubt about it. This is the proper object of faith: but whether it be a *divine* revelation or not, reason must judge; and reason can never permit the mind to reject greater evidence for lesser, nor allow it to entertain probability over certainty. There can be no evidence that any traditional revelation clearer than the principles of reason: and therefore nothing that is contrary to, and inconsistent with, the clear and self-evident dictates of reason, has a right to be urged or assented to as a matter of faith.

If Boundaries aren't set between Faith and Reason, no Extreme Enthusiasm in Religion can be contradicted. If faith and reason aren't kept distinct by boundaries, there will be no room for reason at all in matters of religion; and extravagant opinions and ceremonies found in several religions can't be blamed for anything. This appeal to faith in *opposition* to reason is a good explanation of those absurdities found in almost all the religions that possess and divide mankind.

People who are taught not to consult reason in matters concerning religion, no matter how contradictory to common sense and the very principles of all their knowledge, have let loose superstition, have been led into strange opinions and extravagant practices in religion. A reasonable person can only be amazed at their follies, and judge them as unacceptable to a wise God, and can't avoid thinking of them as ridiculous and offensive. Religion, which should distinguish us from beasts and elevate us above the brutes, is often the area in which men appear most irrational, and more senseless than the beasts themselves.

-John Locke

THE END

Commentary on John Locke

John Locke continued the vein of skeptical thought initiated by Hobbes, stressing the limits of human understanding, the weakness of sensory perception and ridiculing the excesses of 'enthusiasm' in religion. Like many Philosophers of his times, he struggled with the problem of revealed religion and innate knowledge. As a general practitioner and scientist he saw the advantages of empirical proof, trial and error and a cool detached outlook. In politics, he gained first-hand experience in the danger power politics.

His insistence on empirical knowledge entailed some startling questions conclusions: if we are a 'blank slate' at birth, who writes on us? Society with its backwards prejudices? Random encounters? Government propaganda? Who decides who does the writing? Most importantly, can I do the writing myself? Is my life uncharted?

Unlike Hobbes, Locke was a great fan of Rene Descartes, who asked many of the same questions, but who came up with different answers. Descartes thought he could restructure his mind, beginning with the certainty "I think, therefore I am". Locke might answer, "I sense, therefore I am." But it should be remembered that questioning innate (inborn) knowledge hardly went over very well in an agricultural population. Wouldn't a farmer simply pick up a seed and ask how it knew it would become a stalk of corn? By experience? By trial and error? How do animals 'know' how to take care of their young?

John Locke's contributions, especially his role in political philosophy as inspiration to Thomas Jefferson, deserve further study. The implications of his thoughts are far-reaching and form the fabric of our Declaration of Independence, Constitution and Bill of Rights.

PART III
HUME

A Short Biography of David Hume (Born: April 26, 1711. Died August 25, 1776.)

David Hume, our last selection, was born in Edinburgh, Scotland and raised at Ninewells near Berwick after his father died while David was still a child. Around age 13 he entered the University of Edinburgh, and like Hobbes and Hume, was bored with the curriculum and sought out his true interests on the sly. While his family thought he was studying law, he was reading classics. He tried his hand at business, hated it and set off for France, where he spent three adventurous years, penning his first work *Treatise of Human Nature*. It was an unqualified flop. Discouraged, he took inventory and had better luck with *Essays, Moral and Political*. After he failing to obtain a post at the University, he became tutor to Marquis Annandale for a year, who had unfortunately been declared legally insane. Hume's next stop was as an aide-de-camp to General St. Clair, a relative. To his great pleasure this position allowed him to travel in style with the General and save a considerable sum of money.

Returning to England after several diplomatic missions, he used the influence of his friend, the famous economist Adam Smith, to obtain a university post, but to no avail; his reputation as a skeptic had created many enemies. He worked as a librarian, but lost that position for ordering what some staff considered anti-religious texts for the collection.

His major breakthrough came as a historian. His multi-volume *History of England* was such a success that he was chiefly thought of as a Historian during his lifetime. He returned to diplomatic service in 1763 and spent three years in Paris, where the cream of French society dubbed him "Bon David" or Good David. He was a large, jolly fellow fond of food and drink, a darling of the ladies and quick with a joke. The only dark spot of the trip was his short friendship with the paranoid genius J.J. Rousseau. Despite Hume's efforts to aid Rousseau by securing him a pension, the delusional Frenchman was certain Hume was plotting against him!

Later Hume accepted a post as Undersecretary of the Foreign Office, retiring in 1768 to build a new home and enjoy his considerable wealth and friendships. He died in late summer 1776 surrounded by friends and admirers. Before he died news of the Declaration of Independence reached him, and he cheerfully applauded the upstart American colonists.

The main reading below, *Dialogues Concerning Natural Religion* was published three years after his death in 1779 by his loving nephew, after Hume's close friend Adam Smith refused to publish it, finding it too controversial.

Selections from "Dialogues Concerning Natural Religion" and "An Enquiry Concerning the Principles of Morals" by David Hume, Updated, Edited and Modernized by Prof. Les Sutter (copyright of paraphrase, 2003)

In the original Hume used different names, listed below. I have substituted them for more common names to give the text a more natural feel:

Original: Pamhilus = Pam. Chris'(Cleanthes) daughter. The dialogues were intended to instruct her. She represents youth, students and all minds shaped by instruction.

Original: Hermippus = Herb. Friend of Pam (Pamhilus).

Original: Cleanthes = Chris. Pam (Pamhilus) father. His position represents liberal Christianity, a position very close to that of John Locke, favoring sensory reasoning over faith.

Original: Philo = Phil. An unorthodox skeptic. Most academics concur that this character served the purpose of expressing a watered-down version of David Hume's own position, which was far more radical and dangerous during his lifetime.

Original: Demea = Dave. Represents tradition and dogmatic, orthodox theology.

The selection opens with Pam telling Herb about a discussion that took place the previous summer. The format of a dialogue allows Hume the luxury of long rants and counter raves, reading almost like a play, thus retaining the reader's interest longer than a simple polemic might. A second advantage is that diverse viewpoints may be raised within the context of a dialogue; this permits Hume the opportunity to alternately soothe his philosophical opponents by presenting their objections, as well as to and roast caricatures of them in various straw man scenarios. As we shall see, he uses both with relish.

PAM TO HERB

"It's been said, Herb, that ancient philosophers conveyed most of their instruction using dialogues and this method hasn't been used lately, and hasn't done much for those who tried it. Accurate and regular argument is expected of today's philosophers, naturally throws them into methodical and didactic modes; where one can immediately explain the point in question without preparation and proceed without interruption to the necessary proofs. To deliver a 'system' in conversation isn't natural; and as the dialogue-writer, he departs from the direct style of composition (adding a freedom in his performance) avoiding the appearance of author and reader. Still, he is likely to get into trouble and convey the image of teacher and pupil. Or, if he rambles on in the spirit of good company he throws in a variety of topics, allowing everyone a chance to speak his mind, he often loses too much time in preparations and verbal transitions and the reader feels cheated by all the small talk—in the end brevity and precision suffer."

"But you know," continued Pam, "There are some subjects where dialogue writing can be adapted, and where it is still better than the direct method of composition. So here we go."

"Any obvious point of doctrine that hardly anyone makes bones about it, but which is at the same time important, needs a method to handle it. The charm of conversation pushes the point; and hopefully where the personalities and characters aren't tedious or redundant."

"On the other hand any question of philosophy so obscure and uncertain that human reason can't reach a conclusion about it, well, it leads us naturally into the style of dialogue and conversation. Sane men can disagree when one can't be sure about something. Opposite points of view can be amusing if the subject is odd and interesting, so the book carries us into comradeship; and unites two great and pure pleasures of human life, study and society."

"Luckily for us, Herb, all of these circumstances can be found in our subject: Natural Religion. What truth is more obvious, so certain, as the being of God? Even the most ignorant ages have acknowledged it. What truth is more important than this? But in the treatment of this obvious and important truth, obscure questions occur concerning the nature of that Divine Being, his attributes, his decrees, his plan of providence. These have been always subjected to dispute, and human reason hasn't reached any certain determination about them. But these topics are so interesting, that we can't restrain our restless inquiry even though nothing but doubt, uncertainty, and contradiction have been the result of our most accurate researches."

"I observed this when I spent part of the summer season with Chris, where I was present during conversations with Phil and Dave. I told you about them, but it was an imperfect account. You told me that your curiosity was so excited that you wanted me to give you the details, and explain the various systems they used regarding the delicate subject of natural religion. The remarkable contrast in their characters raised your expectations even more; you opposed the accurate philosophical turn of Chris over the careless Skepticism of Phil, or compared either of their dispositions with the rigid, inflexible orthodoxy of Dave. My youth at the time rendered me merely a spectator to their disputes; and my curiosity, natural at that early stage of life deeply imprinted the whole chain of their arguments. I hope I won't omit or confuse any part of them."

—Pam

PART 1

After I joined the group I found sitting in Chris's library, Dave paid Chris some compliments about the great care he took towards my education, and on his tireless perseverance and constancy in regard to all of his friendships.

"Pam's Dad," said Dave, "Was your intimate friend: his son is your pupil; and may be regarded as your own, if were we to judge the relationship by all the trouble you take in conveying every useful branch of literature and science. In my opinion you're not lacking in prudence or industry. Therefore I'll pass along a maxim I've observed regarding my own children, in order to see how it agrees which your experience. The method I follow in their education is founded on the saying of an ancient, 'That students of philosophy ought first to learn logic, then ethics, then physics, last of all the nature of the gods'."

"According to him the science of natural theology is the most profound them all, requiring the most mature judgment in students and only those minds enriched with all the other sciences can safely study it."

"Did you wait that long," says Phil, "To teach your children the principles of religion? Isn't there a danger of their neglecting or rejecting wholesale religious opinions that they heard so little about during the whole course of their education?"

"It's only as a science," replied Dave, "Subjected to human reasoning and disputation, that I postponed the study of Natural Theology. To season their minds with early on with piety is my major concern. Using continual instruction and my own example I've deeply imprinted their tender minds with reverence for the principles of religion. As they pass through other sciences, I notice the uncertainty, the eternal disputations, the obscurity of philosophy and the strange conclusions which some of the greatest geniuses have derived from the principles of human reason. Having tamed their minds into a proper submission I no longer have any scruples about teaching them the greatest mysteries of religion; nor do I expect any danger from philosophy, which may lead them to reject firmly established doctrines and opinions."

"Your precaution," said Phil, "Of seasoning your children's minds early with piety, is certainly very reasonable; and is necessary in this irreligious age. But what I chiefly admire in your plan of education is your method of drawing the advantages from the principles of philosophy and learning. In every age, inspiring pride and self-sufficiency has usually been destructive to the principles of religion. Those who are unacquainted with science and profound questions, observe the endless disputes of the learned, and become filled with contempt for philosophy. Then they rivet themselves tightly to in the major points of theology they've been taught."

"Those who study and inquire a little find much evidence in new and extraordinary doctrines and think nothing is beyond human reason. They presumptuously break through all barriers to the inmost sanctuaries of the temple. But I hope Chris will agree with me that after we've abandoned ignorance, there's still another possibility to prevent profane excesses."

"Let Dave's principles be improved and cultivated. Let's become thoroughly aware of the weakness, blindness, and narrow limits of human reason. Let's duly consider its uncertainty and endless contraries, even in daily life and practices. Let the errors and deceits of our senses be placed in front of us: the difficulties which accompany the first principles in all systems; the contradictions which adhere to the very ideas of matter, cause and effect, extension, space, time, motion; and in a word, quantity of all kinds, the object of the only science that can fairly pretend to any certainty or evidence. When these topics are displayed in a clear light, which they are by some philosophers and almost all clergymen, who can remain confident in this weak faculty of reason and pay any regard to its conclusions in points so sublime from daily life?"

While Phil uttered these words, I observed a smile from both Dave and Chris. Dave's seemed to imply an unreserved satisfaction in the doctrines. But, in Chris's features I could distinguish an air of finesse; as if he perceived some artificial malice in Phil's reasoning.

"So, Phil, you propose," said Chris, "To base religious faith on philosophical Skepticism? And you think, that if certainty or evidence is expelled from every other subject of inquiry, it will all return to these theological doctrines, and there acquire a superior force and authority? Whether your Skepticism is as absolute and sincere as you think, we'll see! When the discussion breaks up we'll see whether you leave by the door or window! And whether you really doubt if your body has gravity! Or can be injured by its fall! And all this according to popular opinion derived from our fallacious senses, and more fallacious experience! And, Dave, I think this consideration may serve to end our ill will toward this funny sect of Skeptics. If they're really serious they won't trouble the world for long with their doubts and disputes. If they're only kidding they can't be very dangerous, either to the state, to philosophy, or to religion."

"In reality, Phil," he continued, "Even though a man may totally renounce all his beliefs and opinions after intense reflection on the many contradictions and imperfections of human reason, it's impossible for him to continue in total Skepticism, even for a few hours. External objects surround him; passions flare; his philosophic melancholy weakens and even the utmost effort will not be able to preserve the poor appearance of Skepticism for any length of time."

"So why should he do this to himself? It's impossible for him to ever satisfy himself on this point and be consistent with his skeptical principles. So, on the whole, nothing could be more ridiculous than the principles of the ancients; if in reality they actually attempted to spread the Skepticism they learned."

"In this light, there's a great resemblance between the sects of the Stoics and Pyrrhonians. Although constant opponents both of them seem to be founded on the erroneous maxim, 'That what a man can sometimes perform in some dispositions, he can perform always, and in every disposition.' According to the Stoics, when the mind is elevated into a sublime enthusiasm of virtue, and strongly possessed by any type of honor or public good, the sharpest bodily pain and sufferings will not conquer such a strong sense of duty and it's even possible to smile during torture. If this is sometimes actually the case in reality, then while at school or in his study, a philosopher may work himself up to extreme enthusiasm; but how will he maintain this enthusiasm? His mind relaxes, and can't be recalled at will; hobbies distract him, bad luck sneaks up on him and soon the philosopher sinks by degrees into the common man."

"I'll allow you to compare the Stoics and Skeptics," replied Phil, "But at the same time observe that although the mind cannot support the highest flights of philosophy using Stoicism. Even when it sinks lower, it still retains some of its former disposition and the effects of the Stoic's reasoning will appear in his daily conduct, and through all of his actions. The ancient schools, particularly that of Zeno, produced examples of virtue which seem astonishing even today."

"In the same manner, if a man is used to skeptical considerations regarding the uncertain and narrow limits of reason, he won't completely forget them when he reflects on other subjects. In all his philosophic principles and reasoning, I wouldn't say his common conduct will be different from those who either never formed any opinions, or who have opinions more favorable to human reason."

"To whatever length anyone may push the speculative principles of Skepticism, they must act, live, and converse like other men, if for no other reason than the absolute necessity of so doing. If one ever carries their speculations further than this necessity forces, it is because they are attracted by the pleasure and satisfaction found in acting that way. We may also consider that everyone, even in daily life, is forced to have some degree of this philosophy. Beginning in infancy we make continual advances and form more general principles of conduct and reasoning; the greater the experience we acquire, and the stronger the reason we obtain, we will always render our principles more general and comprehensive;

and that what we call philosophy is nothing but a more regular and methodical operation of the same kind. To philosophize on such subjects isn't essentially different from reasoning about daily life. We can expect greater stability and truth from our philosophy due to its more exact and scrupulous method of proceeding."

"But when we look beyond human affairs and their properties and carry our speculations into two eternities, the one before and after the present state of things; into the creation and formation of the universe; the existence and properties of spirits; the powers and operations of one universal Spirit existing without beginning and without end; omnipotent, omniscient, immutable, infinite, and incomprehensible. To do so we must be far removed from the smallest tendency to Skepticism so as not to be apprehensive, because there we are far beyond the reach of our faculties."

"As long as we confine our speculations to business, morals, politics, or other criticism, we make appeals to common sense and experience all the time, which strengthen our philosophical conclusions, and remove the suspicion we entertain with regard subtle and refined reasoning. But, in theological reasoning, we don't have this advantage because we focus on objects which are too large for our grasp."

"We are like foreigners in a strange country, where everything seems suspicious, and every moment we are in danger of transgressing the laws and customs of the people. We don't know how far we ought to trust our methods of reasoning in this subject because in daily life we cannot account for them, and we are thus entirely guided by our instincts."

"All Skeptics maintain that if reason is considered abstractly, it furnishes invincible arguments against itself; and that we could never retain any conviction on any subject if skeptical reasoning weren't so refined and subtle, that it wasn't able to counter natural arguments derived from sensory experience. But it's evident whenever our arguments lose this advantage and stray from daily life, the most refined Skepticism is on an even footing with them, and is able to counteract them. One has no more weight than the other. The mind must remain in suspense between them; and that very suspense is the triumph of Skepticism."

"But I observe Phil," says Chris, "In you and all speculative Skeptics, there is a gap between your doctrine and practice in the points of theory as well as in the conduct of daily life. Wherever evidence is found, you grasp it, despite your Skepticism; and I also observe that some of your ridicule those who make even greater claims to certainty. In reality, wouldn't a man be ridiculous who pretended to reject Newton's explanation of the rainbow, because that explanation gives a minute anatomy of the rays of light; a subject too refined for human comprehension? And what would you say to someone who, having no particular real objection to Copernicus and Galileo, disagrees anyway on the general principle that these subjects were too magnificent to be explained fallacious human reason?"

Chris shifted in his chair and continued.

"There certainly is a brutal and ignorant variety of Skepticism which gives a vulgar person a general prejudice against what they don't easily understand, and makes them reject every principle which requires elaborate reasoning to prove it. This species of Skepticism is fatal to knowledge, but not to religion because we find that those who profess it most, often approve of the great truths of Theism and natural theology, and even to the most absurd tenets suggested by traditional superstition. They firmly believe in witches, but they won't believe simplest of Euclid's propositions! But the refined and philosophic Skeptics fall into inconsistency of a different nature. They research the most obscure corners of science; and their beliefs attend them every step, in proportion to the evidence they encounter. They are even obliged to acknowledge that the most obscure and distant objects are best explained by philosophy."

Chris pointed his finger in no particular direction and leaned forward, eager to press on with his argument while the others listened with increasing interest.

"These Skeptics are obliged to consider particular evidence and gauge their assent to the precise degree of evidence which occurs. This is their practice in all areas of natural, mathematical, moral, and political science. And why not the same in theological and religious questions? Why must conclusions of this nature be rejected on the general presumption of the insufficiency of human reason, without any particular discussion of the evidence? Isn't such unequal conduct plain proof of prejudice?"

"You say our senses are fallacious; our understanding erroneous; our ideas, even of the most familiar objects, extension, duration, motion, full of absurdities and contradictions. You defy me to solve the difficulties you discover in them. I don't have the capacity for such a great undertaking. I don't have the leisure for it. I perceive it to be superfluous. In every circumstance your own conduct refutes your principles, and shows the firmest reliance on all the received maxims of science, morals, prudence, and behavior."

"I'll never agree with the opinion that Skeptics are not a sect of philosophers; they are only a sect of liars. However I may affirm—I hope without offending you—that they are a sect of jesters. But whenever I find myself disposed to amusement, I shall certainly choose a less perplexing and abstruse entertainment. A comedy, a novel, or a history book seems a more natural recreation than such metaphysical subtleties and abstractions."

"In vain would the skeptic make a distinction between science and common life, or between one science and another. The arguments employed are all of a similar nature, and contain the same force and evidence. Or if there is any difference between them, the advantage lies entirely on the side of theology and natural religion! Many principles of mechanics are founded on very abstruse reasoning; still any man who has pretensions to science, not even a speculative skeptic pretends to entertain the least doubt with regard to them! The Copernican system contains the most surprising paradox, contrary to appearances, and to our very senses: yet even monks and inquisitors are now forced to withdraw their opposition to it. And should Phil, a man of extensive knowledge entertain any general undistinguished scruples regarding the religious hypothesis, founded on simple and obvious arguments? And unless it meets artificial obstacles, it has such an easy admission into the mind."

"And here we may observe," he continued, turning himself towards Dave, "A pretty strange turn in the history of science. After a union of philosophy with a popular religion, that is early Christianity, nothing was more usual among all their religious teachers than declamations against reason, against the senses, against every principle derived only from human research and inquiry."

"All the topics of the ancient academics were adopted by the Church fathers; and then taught for several ages in every school and pulpit throughout Christendom. The Protestants embraced the same principles of reasoning and all the sermons on the excellency of faith were interlaced with some severe satire against natural reason."

"John Locke seems to have been the first Christian who ventured openly to assert, that faith was nothing but a species of reason; that religion was only a branch of philosophy; and that a chain of arguments, similar to that which established any truth in morals, politics, or physics, was always employed in discovering all the principles of theology, natural and revealed. The poor use of philosophical Skepticism by the Church fathers and first reformers further propagated the sentiments of Mr. Locke. It is now widely regarded by all amateurs in reasoning and philosophy, that an Atheist and a Skeptic are almost synonymous! And as it's certain that no man is serious when he professes the latter principle, I hope there are few who seriously maintain the former".

"Don't you remember," said Phil, "The excellent saying by Lord Francis Bacon on this?"

"Yes," replied Chris, "That a little philosophy makes a man an Atheist, a great deal converts him to religion."

"That's a very judicious remark too." said Phil. "But what I have in mind is another passage, where, having mentioned David's fool, who said in his heart there is no God, this great philosopher observes, that the Atheists nowadays have a double share of folly; for they are not contented to say in their hearts there is no God, but they also utter that impiety with their lips, and are thereby guilty of multiplied indiscretion and imprudence. Such people, though they were serious, I can't imagine them to be very formidable."

"Although you might include me in this class of fools, I can't resist making a remark that occurs to me, from the history of religious and irreligious Skepticism. It smells strongly of priests in the whole progress of this affair. During the dark ages which followed the dissolution of the ancient schools, the priests perceived that Atheism, Deism, or heresy of any kind, could only proceed from questioning religious opinions, and from a belief that human reason was a measure of everything."

"Dogma had a strong influence over the minds of men, and was almost equal to suggestions of the senses and common sense, which governed even the most determined skeptic. But today the influence of dogma is diminished, and men, more open to the world, compare the principles of different nations and ages. If we distrust human reason, we have now no other principle to lead us into religion. Skeptics in one age, dogmatists in another; the clergy uses whichever system best suits their purpose of gaining control over mankind. It is sure to be their favorite principle, and established tenet."

"It's very natural," said Chris with some satisfaction, "For men to embrace those principles that best defend their doctrines."

PART 2

"I must confess Chris," said Dave, "That nothing surprises me more than the light in which you've put this argument. By the tone of your discourse, one would imagine that you were maintaining the Being of a God against Infidels and were a champion of that fundamental principle of all religions. But I hope this isn't a question between us. No man of common sense ever entertained a serious doubt with regard to a truth so certain and self-evident."

"The question," he continued, "Doesn't concern the being, but the nature of God. But don't think that my piety has got the better of my philosophy! I shall support my opinion as needed. I might cite all the greats, from the foundation of Christianity, who have ever treated of this or any other theological subject."

"But surely, Dave," said Phil, "Where reasonable men treat these subjects, the question can never be concerning the Being, but only the nature of the Deity. The former truth, as you well observe, is unquestionable and self-evident. Nothing exists without a cause, and the original cause of this universe (whatever it be) we call God and piously ascribe to him every type of perfection. He is infinitely superior to our limited comprehension and he is more likely the object of worship in a temple, than a subject of academic disputation."

"In reality, Chris," he continued, "There is no need of having recourse to that affected Skepticism so displeasing to you, in order to come at this determination. Our ideas reach no further than our experience. We have no experience of divine attributes and operations. I needn't conclude my syllogism. You can draw the inference yourself! And it's a pleasure for me (and I hope to you too) that reasoning and piety concur with the conclusion, and both of them establish the mysterious and incomprehensible nature of the Supreme Being."

"Let's not lose any time in circumlocutions," said Chris, addressing himself to Dave, "Much less in replying to Phil's pious declamations. I'll briefly explain how I look at this matter. Look around the world. Contemplate the whole, and every part of it. You'll find it's nothing but one big machine, admired by everyone who ever contemplated it."

"I'll tell you, Chris," said Dave, "That from the beginning, I couldn't approve of your conclusions and even less of the ways in which you establish them. What! No demonstration of the Being of God? No abstract arguments? No proofs a priori! Are these, insisted upon by philosophers, all sophism? Can we go no further in this subject than experience and probability? I won't say that this is betraying the cause of a Deity: but surely, you're giving advantages to Atheists, which they never could obtain by argument and reasoning!"

"My chief concern in this subject," said Phil, "Is not so much that Chris reduces all religious arguments are reduced to experience, but more that they don't appear to be the most certain of that inferior kind. That a stone will fall, that fire will burn, that the earth has solidity, yes, we've all observed thousands of times. When any new instance of this nature is presented, we draw the accustomed inference. The exact similarity of the cases gives us a perfect assurance of a similar event; and stronger evidence is never desired nor sought."

"If we see a house, Chris, we conclude that it had an architect or builder; because this is precisely the effect we have experienced to proceed from that cause. But surely you won't affirm that the universe bears such a resemblance to a house? That we can infer a similar cause, or that the analogy here is perfect? The differences are so striking, that the most you can assume is a presumption concerning a similar cause; and how that pretension will be received by others, I leave to you."

"It would be poorly received," replied Chris, "And I deserve blame if I meant that the proofs of a Deity amounted to no more than a guess or conjecture. But is the whole adjustment of 'means to ends' in a house, and in the universe so far off? The economy of final causes?"

"Good God!" cried Dave, interrupting him, "Where are we? Zealous defenders of religion admit that the proofs of a Deity fall short of perfect evidence! And you, Phil, I depended on your assistance in proving the adorable mysteriousness of the Divine Nature, do you assent to all of Chris' extravagant opinions? What else can I call them? Why should I spare my censure when such principles are advanced, supported by such an authority, before a person as young as Pam?"

"You don't seem understand." replied Phil, "I argue with Chris in his own way. By showing him the dangerous consequences of his points, I hope to finally swing him over to our beliefs. But what sticks with you most is the representation Chris made of the argument 'a posteriori'. Finding that that argument is likely to vanish into thin air, you think it's so disguised, that you can't believe its set in its true light. Now, however much I may dissent in other respects from the dangerous principles of Chris, I must admit he has fairly represented that argument."

"I am, however, scandalized by the resemblance asserted between the Deity and human creatures; it implies a degradation of the Supreme Being. With your assistance, Dave, I will try to defend what you call the adorable mysteriousness of Divine Nature, and will attempt to refute Chris' reasoning, if he allows me to…"

Chris agreed. After a short pause Phil proceeded in the following manner.

"Chris, I won't dispute that all inferences concerning facts are founded on experience. Nor that all experimental reasoning is founded on the supposition that similar causes prove similar effects, and similar effects similar causes. But I ask you to observe the extreme caution all good thinkers use when transferring experiments to similar cases! Unless the cases are exactly similar, they lack perfect confidence in applying there past observation to any particular phenomenon. Every change of circumstances creates a doubt concerning the event; and it requires new experiments to prove that the new circumstances are of no importance. A change in any particulars may result in the most unexpected consequences. The slow and deliberate steps of philosophers are distinguished from the march of the vulgar, which are hurried and incapable of all consideration."

"So far from admitting," continued Phil, "That the operations of a part can afford us any just conclusion concerning the origin of the whole, I won't allow any one part to form a rule for another part, if the latter be very remote from the former. Is there any reasonable ground to conclude, that the inhabitants of other planets possess thought, intelligence, reason, or any thing similar to these faculties in men? When nature has so extremely diversified her manner of operation in this small globe, can we imagine that she incessantly copies herself throughout so immense a universe? A very small part of this great system, during a very short time, is very imperfectly discovered to us; and do we thence pronounce decisively concerning the origin of the whole?"

"And Chris, can you blame me if I add the noted story of the philosopher who, after being asked 'What was God?' asked for a day to think of it, and then two more days more, and continually prolonged the term, without ever bringing in his definition or description? Could you blame me, if I had answered, that I didn't know, and that this subject lay vastly beyond my reach? You might cry out "Skeptic!" but the imperfections of human reason allow no success on a subject so sublime and remote from our observation. When two species of objects have always been observed to be together, I can infer by habit the existence of one wherever I see other. This is an argument from experience. But how can this argument take place, where the objects are individual, without parallel, or specific resemblance?"

Phil was proceeding in this vehement manner, somewhat between jest and earnest, as it appeared to me, when he observed some signs of impatience in Chris, and then immediately stopped short.

"What I suggested," said Chris, "Is only that you stop abusing terms, or popular expressions, to subvert philosophical reasoning. You know the vulgar often distinguish reason from experience, even where the question relates only to matter of fact and existence. But when the reason is properly analyzed, it is nothing but a species of experience. To prove the origin of the universe from experience is no more contrary to common speech, than to prove the motion of the earth from the same principle. And one might raise the same objections to the Copernican system, which you have urged against my reasoning. Have you seen other earths move? Have…"

"Yes!" cried Phil, interrupting him, "We have other earths. Isn't the moon another earth, which we've seen turning round? Isn't Venus another earth, where we observe the same phenomenon? Aren't the revolutions of the sun also a confirmation, from analogy, of the same theory?"

"In reality, Chris," he continued, "The modern system of astronomy has become such an essential part of our education that we don't examine its foundations. It's now merely a matter of curiosity to study the first writers on that subject, who encountered the full force of prejudice, and were obliged to twist their arguments every possible way to render them popular and convincing."

"In the cautious nature of the astronomers, you can see your own condemnation, Chris. Or rather, see that the subject exceeds all human reason and inquiry. Can you pretend to show any such similarity between a house, and the generation of a universe? Have you ever seen nature in resemble the first arrangement of the elements? Have worlds ever been formed in front of you? Have you had the leisure to observe the whole progress of the phenomenon, from creation to final consummation? If you have, then cite your experience, and deliver your theory."

PART 3

"Amazing how the most absurd argument may acquire an air of probability," replied Chris, "In the hands of a man of ingenuity and invention! Phil, aren't you aware that it became necessary for Copernicus to prove the similarity of the terrestrial and celestial matter because several philosophers denied this similarity? But isn't it necessary that Theists should prove the similarity of nature to design because the similarity is self-evident?"

"Let me observe," continued Chris, "That the religious argument, instead of being weakened by Skepticism, rather acquires force from it, and becomes more firm and undisputed. To exclude all reasoning of any kind is madness. The declared profession of every reasonable skeptic is only to reject remote arguments, to adhere to common sense and to agree whenever reasons strike him with such force that he can't disagree. Now the arguments for Natural Religion are plainly like this; and nothing but perverse metaphysics can reject them. Consider the eye; survey its structure and tell me, doesn't the idea of a designer immediately enter your mind? The most obvious conclusion is in favor of design! But it requires time, reflection, and study to summon objections which support Infidelity. To what degree of blind dogmatism must one have to reject such natural and such convincing arguments on nature?"

"It sometimes happens, I admit, that religious arguments have no influence on a barbarian because he never asks himself any question about them. Why does an animal have a strange shape? From its parents. And their shape? From their parents? And so on, until the objects at such a distance, that they are lost in darkness and confusion. And he lacks any curiosity to trace them further. But this is neither dogmatism nor Skepticism, but stupidity: a state of mind very different from your sifting, inquisitive disposition, my ingenious friend! You trace causes from effects. You compare the most distant and remote objects. Your greatest errors don't come from barrenness of thought and invention, but from too much thinking, which suppresses your natural good sense and by a profusion of unnecessary objections!"

Here I could observe, Herb, that Phil was a little embarrassed and confounded. While he hesitated in delivering an answer, luckily for him, Dave broke in upon the discourse, and saved his countenance.

"Your instance, Chris," Dave said, "Is drawn from books and language and has so much force. But isn't there some danger in this? Might it render us presumptuous, by making us imagine we comprehend the Deity? That we have some adequate idea of his nature and attributes? When I read a volume, I enter into the mind of the author. I become him for an instant and have an immediate feeling and conception of the ideas in his imagination when he composed. But we can never be this close to the Deity. His ways are not our ways. His attributes are perfect, but incomprehensible. And the book of nature contains a great and inexplicable riddle, far beyond any intelligible discourse."

"The ancient Platonists, you know, were the most religious and devout of all the Pagan philosophers; yet many of them, particularly Plotinus, expressly declare that intellect is not to be ascribed to the Deity. Our perfect worship consists not in acts of veneration, but in mysterious self-annihilation. Perhaps these ideas go too far; but it must be acknowledged that by representing the Deity as intelligible, comprehensible and so similar to a human mind, we are guilty of narrow partiality and make ourselves the model of the whole universe! It seems unreasonable to transfer such sentiments to a supreme existence. All of our ideas, derived from the senses, are false and illusive and cannot therefore occur in a supreme intelligence".

PART 4

"It seems strange to me", said Chris, "That you, Dave, sincere in the cause of religion, still maintain the mysterious, incomprehensible nature of the Deity, and insist strenuously that he has no resemblance to humans. How do you mystics, who maintain the absolute incomprehensibility of the Deity, differ from Skeptics or Atheists, who assert, that the first cause of all is unknown and unintelligible? After rejecting the production by a mind resembling the human mind you assign another specific intelligible cause. You must be very scrupulous indeed, if you refuse to call the universal unknown cause a God or Deity; and to bestow on him the many sublime eulogies and epithets you require of them."

"Who could imagine," replied Dave, "That Chris, the calm philosophical Chris, would attempt to refute his antagonists by affixing nickname on them; and, like the common bigots of the age and resort declamation, instead of reasoning? Or doesn't he perceive, that these topics are easily retorted, as is the epithet of Mystic, with which he has honored us?"

"Chris, consider what you assert when you represent the Deity as similar to a human. What is the soul of man? A composition of various faculties, passions, sentiments, and ideas united into a person, but still distinct from others. When it reasons the ideas arrange themselves in a certain form, preserved but for a moment, only to immediately yield to another arrangement. New opinions, new passions, new affections, new feelings arise, which continually diversify the mental scene in the most rapid succession imaginable. How is this compatible with that perfect immutability and simplicity which all true Theists ascribe to the Deity?"

"They say God sees the past, the present, and the future. His love and hatred, his mercy and justice, are one individual operation. He is in every point in space; and complete in every instant of duration. No succession, no change, no acquisition, no diminution. And what he is this moment he has always been, and ever will be. He is fixed in one simple, perfect state."

"I can allow," said Chris, "That those who maintain the perfect simplicity of the Supreme Being are complete Mystics. They are, in a word, Atheists, without knowing it! For although I allow that the Deity possesses attributes of which we have no comprehension, still we shouldn't ascribe any attributes to him which are incompatible with that intelligent nature essential to him. A mind whose acts and sentiments and ideas are not distinct and successive, that is wholly simple, is a mind which has no thought, no reason, no will, no sentiment, no love, no hatred; or, in a word…is no mind at all! It is an abuse of terms to give it that name!"

"Please consider," said Phil, "Whom you are arguing against. You are honoring Atheists the same as all the orthodox divines who have treated this subject. According to your reckoning, you are the only sound Theist in the world! If idolaters are Atheists, and Christian Theologians the same, what happens to the argument derived from the universal consent of mankind?"

"How shall we satisfy ourselves concerning the cause of the author of the ideal world, into which you trace the material world? Don't we have the same reason to trace that ideal world into another ideal world, or new intelligent principle? But if we stop, and go no further; why go so far? Why not stop at the material world? How can we satisfy ourselves without going on forever? What satisfaction is there in that infinite progression?"

"To say that the different ideas which compose the Supreme Being arrange themselves by their own nature, is talk without any precise meaning. If it has any meaning, why not just say that the material world also arranges itself? I could say that originally everything possessed a faculty of order and proportion, but this is only a more elaborate ways of confessing our ignorance; nor does one hypothesis have any real advantage over another, except in its greater conformity to vulgar prejudices."

"You have presented this argument with a lot of emphasis," replied Chris, "You don't see how easy it is to answer. Even in daily life, if I assign a cause for any event, is it any objection, Phil, that I can't assign the cause of that cause, and answer every new question in such a way? And which philosophers could possibly submit to so rigid a rule? Philosophers, who confess ultimate causes to be totally unknown are aware that the most refined principles they use are just as inexplicable to them as to the average person. The order and arrangement of nature all clearly show an intelligent cause or author. The heavens and the earth say the same thing. All of nature raises one song to the praises of its Creator. You, almost alone, disturb this general harmony! You create doubts and objections! You asked me, what is the cause of the cause? I don't know. I don't care. It doesn't concern me. I have found God and I end my inquiry. If someone wiser or more enterprising wants to go on, let them!"

"I don't pretend to do either," replied Phil. "And for that very reason, perhaps I shouldn't have attempted to go so far; especially when I'm sensible, that I must at last be contented to sit down with the same answer, which, without further trouble, might have satisfied me from the beginning."

PART 5

"But here are a few more inconveniences," continued Phil, "In your Anthropomorphism. Please take an inventory of your principles. Like effects prove like causes. This is the experimental argument, and so you say, the sole theological argument. Now, it's certain, that the more similar the effects presented, and the more similar the causes which are inferred, the stronger the argument. Any departure on either side diminishes the probability, and renders the experiment less conclusive. You can't doubt the principle and you shouldn't reject its consequences."

"All the new discoveries in astronomy, which prove the immense grandeur and magnificence of the works of nature are just so many additional arguments for a Deity according to the true system of Theism. But, according to your hypothesis of experimental Theism, they become so many objections by removing the effect still further from all resemblance to the effects of human art and contrivance."

"The discoveries made by microscopes, even though they open a new universe in miniature, are still objections to you! To me they are arguments in favor of my position. The further we push our researches of this kind, we are still led to infer the universal cause of everything to be vastly different from mankind, or from any object of human experience and observation.

"And what about the discoveries in anatomy, chemistry, botany? These certainly aren't objections," replied Chris. "They only discover new instances of art and contrivance. It is still the image of mind reflected on us from innumerable objects."

"Add a mind like a human," said Phil.

"I don't know any other," replied Chris.

"And the more human the better," insisted Phil.

"Certainly," said Chris.

"Now, Chris," said Phil with an air of triumph, "Look at the consequences. First, by this method of reasoning, you renounce all claims to infinity in any of the attributes of the Deity. As the cause can only be proportioned to the effect, and the effect is not infinite, how can we ascribe it to the Divine Being? You'll still insist that by removing him from all similarity to humans, we give in to an arbitrary hypothesis, and at the same time weaken all proofs of his existence."

"Secondly, you have no reason for ascribing perfection to the Deity, even in his finite capacity. Or for supposing him free from mistakes in his undertakings. There are many difficulties in Nature, which, if we allow a perfect author to be proved a priori, are easily solved, only to become difficulties, because from our narrow capacity we can't trace infinite relations."

He looked briefly out the window, and then turned to face Chris.

"But were this world a perfect production, it still remains uncertain, whether all the work can be attributed a single workman. If we survey a ship, don't we admire the ingenuity of the carpenter who framed so complicated and beautiful a machine? And what a surprise when we find out he's a stupid fellow who imitated others over a long period of time, made multiple mistakes and corrections, only gradually improving his work! Many worlds might have been botched and bungled, throughout an eternity, before our solar system was finally created only after much pointless labor, many fruitless trials, and infinite ages in the art of world-making. Who can determine where the truth or conjecture lies, among a great number of hypotheses on this subject?"

"And what shadow of an argument," continued Phil, "Can you produce, from your hypothesis, to prove the unity of the Deity? A great number of men are required to build a house or ship, so why may not several deities to frame a world? By sharing the work we further limit the attributes of each worker, and get rid of that extensive power and knowledge, which must be supposed in one deity, and which, according to you, can only serve to weaken the proof of his existence."

"In a few words, Chris, a man who follows your hypothesis asserts that the universe arose from design: but that's it. For all he knows this very faulty and imperfect world was only the first crude essay of some infant deity, who later abandoned it, ashamed of his lame performance. It is only the work of some inferior deity, mocked by his superiors. Or is it the production of a senile, superannuated deity? Since his death, perhaps the world has run its own steam from the first impulse it received. I see you are horrified, Dave, at these strange ideas; but these and a thousand more of the same, are really Chris's suppositions, not mine. From the moment the attributes of the Deity are supposed finite, all of this follows. And I can't imagine that such a wild system of theology is preferable to none at all."

"I absolutely disown these ideas!" cried Chris, "And they don't strike me horror, especially when proposed in your rambling manner. On the contrary, they give me pleasure when I see that despite the utmost indulgence of your imagination, you never get rid of the hypothesis of design in the universe. You are always forced to return to it. I continue to regard as a sufficient foundation for religion."

PART 6

"It must be a very weak building," said Dave, "Erected on a tottering foundation because we're uncertain if there's one deity or many; whether they are perfect or imperfect, dead or alive, what confidence can we place in them? How should we address them? What veneration or obedience should we pay to them? To every purpose in life your theory of religion is altogether useless. Even in regard to speculative consequences, its uncertainty renders it totally unsatisfactory."

"To make it still more unsatisfactory," said Phil, "Here's another hypothesis, which must acquire an air of probability from the reasoning insisted on by Chris. That like effects arise from like causes: he considers this principle the foundation of all religion. But there's another principle, no less certain, derived from the same source of experience; where several known circumstances are similar, the unknown will also be found similar. Thus, if we see human limbs, we conclude there is a human head, though hidden from us. If we see a small part of the sun through a hole, we conclude that if the wall were removed, we should see the whole sun. In short, this method of reasoning is so obvious and familiar, that no scruple can ever be made with regard to its solidity."

"You have too much learning, Chris, to be surprised at this opinion which was maintained by almost all the Theists of antiquity. For although the ancient philosophers sometimes reasoned from final causes, as if they thought the world the workmanship of God. Yet it appears their favorite notion was to consider it his body, whose organization renders it subservient to him. And it must be confessed that the universe resembles more a human body than it does the works of human design! If our limited analogy could ever be extended to all of nature, the inference seems to favor the ancients more than modern theory."

"I admit this theory," replied Chris, "While a pretty natural one, has never occurred to me before; but I can't offer an opinion on it on such short notice."

"You are very scrupulous, indeed," said Phil, "If I were to examine any system of yours, I wouldn't have acted with half that caution in starting objections and difficulties. However, if anything occurs to you, I hope you'll let us know."

"Why then!" replied Chris, "It seems to me, that, although the world does resemble an animal body the analogy is defective in many circumstances. Here are the most material: no organs of sense; no seat of thought or reason; no one precise origin of motion and action. In short, it seems to bear a stronger resemblance to a vegetable than to an animal, and your inference would be so far inconclusive in favor of the soul of the world."

"Ancient learning and history seem to have been in great danger of perishing entirely after attacks by barbarians. Had these continued a little longer and been a little more violent, we probably wouldn't have known what happened a few centuries ago. No, if it weren't for the superstition of the Popes who preserved a little jargon of Latin in order to support the appearance of an ancient and universal church, that tongue would have been utterly lost. The Western world would not have been fit for receiving Greek teachings conveyed to them after the sack of Constantinople. When learning and books had been extinguished, even the mechanical arts would have fallen considerably to decay; and it is easily imagined that fables and myths might attribute a much later origin, rather than the true historical one. The against the eternity of the world therefore seems a little precarious."

He paused briefly, and then continued in a thoughtful manner.

"But there appears to be the foundation of a better argument. When cherry trees were first brought from Asia to Europe they were found to thrive so well that in many European climates they grow in the woods without any cultivation. Is it possible, that throughout an eternity, no European passed into Asia and thought of transplanting it into his own country? Empires may rise and fall, but the cherry-tree will still remain in the woods of Greece, Spain, and Italy and will never be affected by the revolutions of human society."

"Less than two thousand years ago, vines were transplanted into France, and there is no climate in the world more favorable to them. Three centuries haven't passed since horses, cows, sheep, swine and dogs were known in America. Is it possible, that during the revolutions of a whole eternity, there never arose a Columbus, who might open the communication between Europe and that continent? We might imagine that all men would wear shoes for ten thousand years, and never have the sense to think of shoelaces to tie them. All these seem convincing proofs of the infancy of the world. Nothing less than a total disaster will ever destroy all the European animals and vegetables which are now to be found in the Western world."

"And what argument do you have against such a disaster happening?" replied Phil, "And if I were obliged to defend any particular system of this nature, which I'd never willingly do, I'd value none more than that which ascribes an eternal inherent principle of order to the world. None of these systems, Skepticism, Polytheism, and Theism has any advantage over the others, according to you. You may thus learn the fallacy of your principles."

PART 7

"But," continued Phil, "In examining the ancient system of 'world soul' it strikes me that you must subvert all of your reasoning and inferences. If the universe bears a greater likeness to animal bodies and vegetables than to humans, it is more probable that its cause resembles the cause of animals and vegetables rather than to reason or design. Your conclusion is therefore lame and defective."

"I hope you'll clear up this argument a little further," said Dave, "Because I don't really understand it in the concise manner in which you expressed it. How is it conceivable that the world can arise from anything similar to vegetation or generation?"

"Very easily." replied Phil, "In the ways a tree sheds its seeds into the neighboring fields, and produces other trees; so the great vegetable, the Earth, or this planetary system, produces within itself seeds, scattered into the surrounding chaos, vegetate into new worlds. A comet, for instance, is the seed of a world; and after it has been fully ripened, by passing from sun to sun, and star to star, is finally tossed into the unformed elements which surround this universe everywhere, and immediately sprouts up into a new system."

"I understand you," says Dave, "But what wild, arbitrary assumptions! What data exists for such extraordinary conclusions? And is the slight, imaginary resemblance of the world to a vegetable or an animal sufficient to establish the same inference with regard to both? Objects which are in general so widely different, should they to be a standard for each other?"

"Right!" cries Phil, "This is the topic on which I've insisted all along! I still assert, that we have no data to establish any system of cosmogony. Our experience, so imperfect in itself, and so limited both in extent and duration, won't allow us probable conjecture concerning the whole of things. Doesn't a plant or an animal, which springs from vegetation or generation, bear a stronger resemblance to the world, than does any artificial machine, which arises from reason and design?"

"But what is this vegetation and generation you're talking about?" said Dave, "Can you explain their operations and the fine internal structure they depend upon?"

"At least as much," replied Phil, "As Chris can explain the operations of reason, or their dependent internal structure. But without any such elaborate assumptions, when I see an animal I infer that it sprang from generation; and I do that with as great a certainty as you conclude a house to have been reared by design."

"But I think," said Dave, "If the world had a vegetative quality, and could sow the seeds of new worlds into the infinite chaos, this power would be still an additional argument for design in its author. How could such a wonderful faculty arise except 'from design'? Or how can order spring from anything which can't perceive that very order it bestows?"

"You only need to look around," replied Phil, "To satisfy yourself on this question. A tree bestows order and organization on that tree which springs from it, without knowing the order; an animal in the same manner on its offspring. To say that all this order in animals and vegetables proceeds ultimately from design, is begging the question."

"Compare he consequences on both sides. The world, say I, resembles an animal; therefore it is an animal, therefore it arose from generation. The steps, I confess, are wide; yet there is some small appearance of analogy in each step. The world, says Chris, resembles a machine; therefore it is a machine, therefore it arose from design. The steps are here equally wide, and the analogy less striking. Reason, in innumerable instances, is observed to arise from generation, but never from any other principle."

PART 8–9

"I shall begin with observing," said Phil, "That there is an evident absurdity in pretending to demonstrate a matter of fact, or to prove it by any arguments a priori. Nothing is demonstrable, unless the contrary implies a contradiction. Nothing, that is distinctly conceivable, implies a contradiction. Whatever we conceive as existing, we can also conceive as non-existent. There is no being whose non-existence implies a contradiction. Consequently there is no being, whose existence is demonstrable. I propose this argument as entirely decisive, and am willing to rest the whole controversy upon it."

"It is said that the Deity is a necessarily existent being; and this necessity of his existence is explained by asserting that if we knew his whole essence or nature, we should perceive it to be as impossible for him not to exist. But this can never happen. It will still be possible for us, at any time, to conceive the non-existence of what we formerly conceived to exist. Thus the words 'necessary existence' have no meaning."

"Add to this, that in tracing an eternal succession of objects, it seems absurd to inquire for a general cause or first author. How can any thing, that exists from eternity, have a cause, since that relation implies a priority in time, and a beginning of existence?"

"But dropping all these abstractions", continued Phil, "and confining ourselves to more familiar topics, I'd add that the argument a priori has seldom been found very convincing, except to people of a metaphysical inclination, who have accustomed themselves to abstract reasoning. Other people of good sense and inclined to religion feel some deficiency in such arguments, although they aren't able to explain it through reasoning."

PART 10

"In my opinion," replied Dave, "Each man somehow feels the truth of religion in his own heart, rather than from reason, and is led to seek protection from God."

"I'm persuaded," said Phil, "That the best and only method of bringing every one to a due sense of religion, is by representations of the misery and wickedness of men."

"People, indeed," replied Dave, "Are sufficiently convinced the miseries of life, the unhappiness of man and the general corruption of our nature. And who can doubt that all men declare this from their own immediate feeling and experience?"

"On this point," said Phil, "The learned agree with the common man; and sacred or profane, the topic of human misery has been the same."

"And why should man," Dave added, "Pretend to an exemption from the lot of all other animals? The whole earth, believe me, Phil, is cursed and polluted. A perpetual war is underway among all living creatures. Necessity, hunger, want, stimulate the strong and courageous: fear, anxiety, terror, agitate the weak and infirm."

"Observe too," said Phil, "The stronger prey upon the weak, and keep them in perpetual terror and anxiety. The weaker too, often prey upon the stronger and molest them without relaxation. Consider insects!"

"I can observe something like what you mentioned," replied Chris, "But I confess I feel little or nothing of it in myself, and hope that it is not so common as you represent it. Ask yourself, or any acquaintance if they would live the last ten or twenty years of their life over again. No! But the next twenty, they say, will be better."

"Old questions remain unanswered. Is God willing to prevent evil, but not able? Then is he impotent. Is he able, but not willing? Then is he cruel. Is he both able and willing? Then what is evil?"

"You have finally," said Chris smiling, "Betrayed your intentions, Phil. Your long agreement with Dave did indeed a little surprise me; but all the time you were preparing arguments against me."

"You take offense easily," replied Dave, "At innocent opinions."

"No!" replied Chris, "No! These arbitrary suppositions can't be true. How can any cause be known but from its effects? How can any hypothesis be proven but from the apparent phenomena? To establish one hypothesis upon another is building on air; and the most we might attain is the bare possibility our opinion; but on such terms we can never establish reality."

"But not to insist upon these topics," continued Phil, "Although obvious and important; I must admonish you, Chris, that you have put the controversy upon a most dangerous issue, and are unawares introducing a total Skepticism into the most essential articles of natural and revealed theology. Here, Chris, I'm really comfortable with my argument. Here I triumph. It is your turn to support your philosophical subtleties against plain reason and experience."

PART 11

"Look around the universe! What an immense profusion of beings! You admire this. But closely inspect these living existences, the only beings worth regarding. How hostile and destructive to each other! How unhappy! How contemptible to the spectator! The whole presents nothing but the idea of blind Nature, without parental care, ignoring her maimed and abortive children!"

"What I have said concerning natural evil will apply to moral evil with little or no variation. We have no more reason to infer that the rectitude of the Supreme Being resembles human rectitude, than that his benevolence resembles the human. No, rather that we have still greater cause to remove moral sentiments, such as we feel them, from God since moral evil is more predominant than moral good, and natural evil more than natural good."

"Stop! Stop!" cried Dave, "Where is your imagination leading you? I joined in alliance with you to refute the principles of Chris, but I now find you running into all the topics of the greatest disbelievers, and betraying our holy cause. Are you secretly a more dangerous enemy than Chris himself?"

"And are you so late in perceiving it?" replied Chris. "Believe me, Dave, your friend Phil, has been amusing himself at both our expense; and it must be confessed, our vulgar theology has given him fuel for ridicule. The total infirmity of human reason, the absolute incomprehensibility of the Divine Nature, the great and universal misery and still greater wickedness of men are strange topics to be cherished by orthodox doctors. In ages of stupidity and ignorance, indeed, these principles may be safely espoused; and perhaps no views of things are more proper to promote superstition, than such as encourage the blind amazement, the diffidence, and melancholy of mankind. But at present…"

"Don't blame," interposed Phil, "The ignorance of these reverend gentlemen. They know how to change their style with the times. Formerly it was a most popular theological topic to maintain, that human life was vanity and misery, and to exaggerate all the ills and pains that are incident to men. But later we find they begin to retract this position; and maintain, though still with some hesitation, that there are more goods than evils, more pleasures than pains, even in this life. When religion stood entirely upon temper and education, it was thought proper to encourage sorrow. But now men have learned to form principles, and to draw consequences, it is necessary to make use of new arguments that will endure some scrutiny and examination."

Phil continued in this spirit of opposition, and his censure of established opinions. But I could observe that Dave didn't relish this part of the discourse at all; soon afterwards he created a pretext to leave.

PART 12

After Dave left, Chris and Phil continued the conversation in the following manner.

"I'm afraid our friend," said Chris, "Will have little inclination to revive this topic when you are around; and to tell you the truth, Phil, your spirit of controversy, joined with your abhorrence of common superstition, carries you such lengths in an argument that nothing sacred and venerable is spared on that occasion."

"I must confess," replied Phil, "That I'm less cautious on the subject of natural religion than on any other. But only because I know that I can never corrupt the principles of any man of common sense and because I'm sure that no one who knows me as man of common sense will ever mistake my intentions. You in particular, Chris, with whom I'm very close, you are aware, that despite the freedom of my conversation, and my love of singular arguments, no one has a deeper sense of religion, or more adores the Divine Being as discovered through reason, than I do."

Chris nodded in agreement and Phil continued.

"Should I meet with a philosophical Atheist, I would ask him: Supposing there were a God, who didn't reveal himself directly to our senses—is it possible for him to give stronger proof of his existence, than the whole face of nature? What could such a Divine Being do except copy the present state of things and make many of his designs so plain that no stupidity could mistake them? Or grant glimpses of still greater creations, which demonstrate his superiority beyond our narrow apprehensions as such imperfect creatures? Now, according to the rules of reasoning, every fact must pass for undisputed, when it is supported by all the arguments its nature admits, even though these arguments aren't numerous or strong. How much more so in the present case where no human imagination can compute their number, and no understanding estimate their strength!"

"I'd like to add," said Chris, "To what you have urged, that one advantage of the principle of Theism is that it can be rendered intelligible and complete. But no system at all, in opposition to a theory supported by reason and by early education, I think it's absolutely impossible to maintain or defend."

"And here I must also acknowledge, Chris," said Phil, "That as the works of Nature have a much greater analogy, we have reason to infer, that the natural attributes of the Deity have a greater resemblance to those of men, than his morals have to human virtues. But what is the consequence? Nothing except that the moral qualities of man are more defective in their kind than his natural abilities."

"My inclination," replied Chris, "Lies in a contrary way. Religion, however corrupted, is still better than no religion at all. The doctrine of a heaven and hell is a strong and necessary safeguard to morals; we shouldn't abandon or neglect it. For if finite and temporary rewards and punishments have such a great effect, how much stronger are infinite and eternal rewards and punishments?"

Phil shook his head in disagreement.

"If," said Phil, "Vulgar superstition are so beneficial to society, why does history abound with so many accounts of its negative consequences on public affairs?"

"The reason," replied Chris, "Is obvious. The proper office of religion is to regulate the heart of men, humanize their conduct, infuse the spirit of temperance, order and obedience..."

"And so will all religion," interrupted Phil, "Except the philosophical and rational kind. Your reason is more easily eluded than my facts. The inference is not just, because finite and temporary rewards and punishments have so great influence, that therefore such as are infinite and eternal must have so much greater."

"The bad effects of such habits, are easily imagined; but where the interests of religion are concerned, no morality can be forcible enough to bind the zealot. The sacredness of the cause sanctifies every measure that can be made use of to promote it. The steady attention alone to eternal salvation, will extinguish benevolence, and beget a narrow, contracted selfishness. And when a zealot's temper is encouraged, it easily eludes all the general precepts of charity and benevolence. Thus, vulgar superstition has no great influence on general conduct; nor is it favorable to morality where it predominates."

"Is there any maxim in politics more certain and infallible, than that both the number and authority of priests should be confined within very narrow limits;

and that the civil magistrate ought to always keep political power out of such dangerous hands?"

"Take care, Phil!" replied Chris, "Take care don't push matters too far. Don't allow your zeal against false religion to undermine your veneration for the true and its comforts."

"These comforts," said Phil, "Are engaging; and with regard to the true philosopher, they are more than appearances. But here the appearances are deceitful, and the terrors of religion commonly prevail above its comforts. I grant that men quickly turn to religion when dejected with grief or depressed with sickness. Isn't this proof that the religious spirit isn't allied to joy, but to sorrow?"

"But afflicted persons find consolation in religion." replied Chris.

"Sometimes." said Phil, "It's true, both fear and hope enter into religion; because both agitate the human mind. But when a man is in a cheerful disposition, he is fit for business, or company, or entertainment of any kind; and he naturally applies himself to these, and doesn't think of religion. When dejected, he has nothing to do but brood upon the terrors of the invisible world, and to plunge himself even deeper into sorrow."

"Being a learned philosophical Skeptic is the first and most essential step towards being a sound, believing Christian. I would recommend this to Pam. And I hope Chris will forgive me for imposing on the education of his pupil."

Note from Pam: Chris and Phil didn't pursue this conversation much further. And after a serious review of everything said, I can only say that Phil's principles are more probable than Dave's; but those of Chris are nearer the truth.

THE END

A selection from: AN ENQUIRY CONCERNING THE PRINCIPLES OF MORALS

By David Hume

OF THE GENERAL PRINCIPLES OF MORALS.

Disputes with men who are obstinate in their principles are the most bothersome except perhaps with those who don't really believe the opinions they defend, but who engage controversy because they desire to show superior wit and ingenuity. The same blind adherence to their own arguments is to be expected in both; the same contempt of their antagonists; and the same passionate sophistry and falsehood. And as reasoning isn't the source their tenets; it's pointless to expect that any logic which doesn't appeal to their ends will ever engage them to embrace sounder principles.

Those who have denied the reality of morality may be ranked among the worst disputants; and it isn't conceivable that any human creature could ever seriously believe that all personalities and actions are all entitled to respect of everyone. The difference which nature has created between persons is so wide, and this difference is further widened by education, example and habit. When these opposite extremes come together there isn't Skepticism so scrupulous, and hardly any assurance so determined, that could absolutely deny any distinction between them. Let a man's insensibility be great, still he must often be touched by right and wrong; and let his prejudices be stubborn, he still must observe that others are capable of similar impressions. The only way of converting an opponent of this kind is to leave him alone. When he finds that nobody is willing to engage in controversy with him, it's probable he will finally grow weary of himself give in to common sense and reason.

Recently there's been a controversy worthy of examination concerning the general foundation of morals; whether they're derived from reason or from emotion; whether we learn them by a chain of argument and induction, or by a immediate intuition; whether, like all sound judgment of truth and falsity, they should be the same to every rational intelligent being; or whether, like the perception of beauty and deformity, they are founded entirely on the constitution of humanity.

Although the ancient philosophers often affirm that virtue is nothing but conformity to reason, in general they still seem to consider morals as arising from taste and emotions.

On the other hand, although modern enquirers talk a great deal about the beauty of virtue and deformity of vice, they commonly try to account for these distinctions by metaphysical reasoning and deductions from abstract principles of understanding. Such confusion reined that opposition to one system in part or in whole could succeed and nobody, till now, made sense of it. The elegant Lord Shaftesbury, first remarked on this distinction, although he himself wasn't entirely free from this confusion.

It must be acknowledged, that both sides of the question have weak arguments. Moral distinctions may be discernible by pure reason: otherwise, why so many disputes in daily life and philosophy regarding the long chain of proofs often produced on both sides; the examples cited, the authorities appealed to, the analogies employed, the fallacies detected, the inferences drawn, and the several conclusions adjusted to their proper principles?

Truth is disputable; not taste: what exists is the standard of judgment; what each man feels within himself is the standard of sentiment. Propositions in geometry may be proved, but the harmony of verse, the tenderness of passion, the brilliancy of wit, is immediate pleasures. No man reasons concerning another's beauty; but frequently concerning the justice or injustice of his actions. In every criminal trial the first object of the prisoner is to disprove the facts alleged, and deny the actions imputed to him: the second to prove, that, even if these actions were real, they might be justified as lawful. It is by deductive understanding that the first point is ascertained: how can we suppose that a different faculty of the mind is employed in the other? On the other hand, those who would resolve all moral determinations into sentiment may try to show, that it is impossible for reason to draw conclusions of this nature. To virtue belongs kindness, to vice, the opposite. This forms their very nature. But can reason or argumentation pronounce beforehand, that this must produce love, and that hatred? Or what other reason can we ever assign for these affections, but the original fabric of the human mind, which is naturally adapted to receive them?

The end of all moral speculations is to teach us our duty; and, by proper representations of the deformity of vice and beauty of virtue, beget habits, and engage us to avoid one and embrace the other. But is this ever to be expected from inferences of understanding, which of themselves can't hold or set in motion the active powers of men? They discover truths: but where the truths which they discover, create no desire, they can't influence conduct and behavior. What is honorable, what is fair, what is becoming, what is noble, what is generous, takes possession of the heart, and animates us to embrace it. What is intelligible, what is evident, what is probable, what is true, procures only the cool assent of the understanding; and gratifying a speculative curiosity, puts an end to our researches.

—David Hume

THE END

Concluding Commentary On Hume and Empiricism

Thomas Hobbes blazed the path, John Locke sought, in his own words, simply to clear away some of the rubbish in the path of human understanding, while David Hume pulled the tablecloth from under the buffet. Hobbes had argued for increased common sense, hands on facts and an end to unsupported superstitious conclusions. His ideal society was founded on a mistrust of human motives, necessarily put in check by a central power. He was a political utilitarian, arguing for an upcoming separation of church and state. Deep down, Hobbes considered human nature evil.

Locke demanded a careful examination of what we know, how we know it and where can it take us. His answer was very little, by experience and not very far. Sounding almost pessimistic, he seems to say that despite the clear advantages empirical science has over revealed religion and rationalism, the rope on the anchor of empiricism is awfully short, just long enough for our limited purposes, Locke pleaded for religious toleration in several of his writings because, in his heart of hearts he feared human nature was emotional and irrational in nature, and limited in scope. He became resigned to the 'human condition' and the attendant political turmoil after 'empirical' contact.

David Hume faced many of the same challenges as Hobbes and Locke, but was cut from a different cloth. He had a cheerful disposition, typical Scottish skepticism and wit, and didn't take pointed personal attacks too seriously. He often remarked to enraged self-appointed crusaders against his ideas (and his person) that Philosophy was an interesting way to pass time. Various enemies succeeded in blocking him from academic positions, fearing he would, like Socrates, corrupt the youth. In fact, Hume was so hated by some of his adversaries that guards had to be posted at this grave for several months after his death; yet you couldn't have imagined a sweeter, or more generous man.

It is difficult to gauge the total effects of the three Empiricists paraphrased in this book, and as I have decided not to create yet another volume explaining their ideas, but rather to make their ideas more accessible, I'll end this project with in the hopes that your curiosity will lead you to the encyclopedia, the library or bookstore to find out more now that I've scratched the surface for you. There is so much more!

—Prof. Dr. Les Sutter

0-595-28191-5